Moving Beyond the Page
Parent Manual

Age 5-7

Concept 3
Patterns

Epiphany Curriculum, LLC

Moving Beyond the Page
Parent Manual
Age 5-7 - Concept 3: Patterns

Author
Kim A. Howe, M.S.

Artist
Anne Marie Gaines, Charde Romero, Emily Van Tassel

Editor / Contributor
Lisa McConnell, Karen Brown, M.A., Abi Santmyer, Anna Gray Hart

© 2019 Epiphany Curriculum, LLC
317 S. Broadway St
Linton, ND 58552

Printed in the United States of America
September 2019

Table of Contents

How to Use Moving Beyond the Page
A Note for Parents

Welcome to *Moving Beyond the Page*. This curriculum will provide you with the tools you need to make learning and teaching an exciting experience for you and your child. Our research-based approach to curriculum design will ensure that your child's needs are met and will provide her with opportunities to meet her highest potential. We don't just want to teach your child what she needs to know to progress to the next grade level; we want her to love learning and to become a lifelong learner.

Your child will enjoy engaging in the hands-on activities and working on the projects throughout the curriculum. All lessons are based on state and national standards, so your child will gain the skills and knowledge he needs in each content area. We go far beyond the standards, which are a minimal requirement for what your child should be learning. Learning is so much more than drills and memorization. Your child will be challenged to: think critically and creatively, solve complex problems, become introspective, research topics, develop products, and participate in real-life learning experiences.

The curriculum is designed to be interdisciplinary; math, language arts, spelling, writing, science, and social studies are all integrated. Art and music are also incorporated into most units. Because of this integrated approach, your child will be adept at transferring knowledge from one field to another and will understand how different fields of study are interrelated.

In the Age 5-7 year-old curriculum, your child will explore all subject areas and will be given ample opportunity to practice reading and writing. The curriculum is filled with quality literature to enjoy with your child. Many gifted 5-7 year-old children have mastered reading. If your child is not reading yet, you may choose to supplement the program with a structured reading curriculum that will meet your child's needs.

Many homeschool children are only taught reading, writing, and math during the early years, but a truly comprehensive curriculum will expose them to science and social studies as well. Often these subjects are the most engaging for a young child.

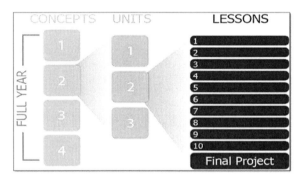

Age 5-7 Curriculum Structure

Curriculum Structure

Your child will explore four concepts that each contain three units. Each unit will last about 3 weeks, so each concept contains about 9 weeks of instruction. The units include: 1.) a vocabulary list, 2.) a shopping list for materials needed in the unit, and 3.) a bibliography for required text and optional literature. Every unit ends with a culminating project where your child will synthesize the knowledge and skills he has gained in the unit. These projects are a great way to assess your child's understanding and knowledge of the content and skills presented in the unit. This form of assessment is much more meaningful and insightful than a traditional test.

Each lesson is presented in an easy-to-use format.

- *Questions to Explore*: these are the big questions related to the concept and ideas in each unit. The lesson will help your child to explore and answer these big questions so that her understanding of the concept is reinforced.
- *Facts and Definitions*: this section outlines the knowledge and vocabulary that your child will learn or memorize in the curriculum. It is not necessary that your child memorize every definition, but it is important that she is exposed to the vocabulary in conversation during the lesson and in other situations.
- *Skills*: These are subjects that your child will practice in the lesson (LA - language arts, S - science, M - Math, SS - social studies). In every lesson your child will learn skills necessary in the different disciplines. Some curricula call these objectives.
- *Materials*: This is a list of all the items and activity pages your child will need to complete the lesson. The materials are simple; most can be found in your home. The activity pages are in the *Student Activity Book*.
- *Introduction*: this where actual instruction begins.
- *Activities*: most lessons include one to four activities for your child to engage in. Some activities include activity pages from the *Student Activity Book*, while others involve hands-on learning experiences such as creating posters, conducting science experiments, using math manipulatives, or acting something out. There are also many activities where you share and discuss stories with your child.
  - Options: Some activities have options. Select the level of the activity appropriate for your child based on her abilities. These are what we call *differentiated* activities.
- *Conclusion*: This often involves summarizing ideas presented in the lesson and asking your child to explain what he has learned in the lesson.

Many lessons also have a handwriting page where your child can practice writing letters, words, or sentences. The letter will correspond with vocabulary words from the lesson. This makes writing letters more meaningful. Students will see that writing serves the purpose of communicating words and ideas. You can decide whether your child needs to practice individual letters, words, or using the words in his own sentence. In addition, we recommend that you implement a reading curriculum based on your child's ability, and we suggest that you spend at least 30 minutes reading aloud to your child.

Daily Schedule	
45-60 minutes	Implementing the lesson plan
30 minutes	Reading and writing instruction
30 minutes	Reading aloud
30 minutes	Math instruction
30 minutes	Physical activity
Optional	
30 minutes	Extend projects based on interest
30 minutes	Re-teach skills not mastered during lesson

Each lesson plan explains in detail what to discuss with your child and how to implement every activity. We have provided flexibility in the schedule, and we encourage you to spend more time on the activities and skills where your child needs more practice, to allow him to explore topics of interest more in-depth, and to extend any project he wishes.

We hope that you and your child will look forward to Moving Beyond the Page each day. It will be a wonderful time of learning and exploration for both of you. You will be preparing your child to become an independent thinker, problemsolver, creative thinker, and innovator, as well as ensuring that he is practicing the important skills required to

Required Books

Unit 1: Identifying and Creating Visual Patterns

☐ *Busy Bugs: A Book About Patterns* by Jayne Harvey

Supplemental Literature

☐ *Pattern (Math Counts)* by Henry Arthur Pluckrose

☐ *Sylvia Long's Mother Goose* by Sylvia Long

Unit 2: Patterns in Sounds, Words, and Actions

☐ *Bear Hugs* by Karma Wilson and Suzanne Watts

Supplemental Literature

☐ *A Child's Garden of Verses* by Robert Louis Stevenson

☐ *Clap Your Hands* by Lorinda Bryan Cauley

☐ *Pattern Bugs* by Trudy Harris

☐ *Pattern Fish* by Trudy Harris

Unit 3: Patterns in Your World

☐ *Pattern* by Henry Pluckrose

Supplemental Literature

☐ *Patterns Everywhere* by Julie Dalton

☐ *Zoe's Hats: A Book of Colors and Patterns* by Sharon Layne Holm

Materials List

The following list of materials will be used over the course of this unit.

Unit 1: Identifying and Creating Visual Patterns

Common Materials

☐ Scissors

☐ markers or crayons

☐ glue or tape

☐ Unifix cubes or Legos

☐ strips of yellow and green construction paper

☐ Legos

☐ Zip-lock bags

☐ thick paper or foam

☐ Caterpillar Patterns game

☐ attribute blocks

☐ materials to make a variety of patterns

☐ letters "A" and "B" cut out of paper

☐ green construction paper

☐ pennies and nickels

☐ lined paper

☐ counting bears or small items such as Legos, pennies, paper clips, or beads

Lesson 1: What Is a Pattern?

☐ strips of red and blue construction paper

☐ tape or glue

Lesson 2: Recognizing Types of Patterns

☐ beads or coins* (2.3 - optional)

Lesson 3: What Comes Next?

© Copyright 2019 Epiphany Curriculum, LLC

Do not copy or distribute without written permission from Epiphany Curriculum, LLC.

Page 6

Unit 1: Identifying and Creating Visual Patterns

- ☐ black marker
- ☐ squares cut out of two colors of construction paper
- ☐ glue

Lesson 4: Extending a Pattern
- ☐ crayons, markers, colored pencils
- ☐ paper clips
- ☐ forks and spoons
- ☐ red construction paper

Lesson 5: Making Color Patterns
- ☐ cookie sheet
- ☐ large macaroni
- ☐ rubbing alcohol
- ☐ tape* (5.2 - optional)
- ☐ food coloring
- ☐ paper towels
- ☐ solid colored dot/circle stickers
- ☐ yarn or twine

Lesson 6: Shapes and Patterns
- ☐ red, yellow, and blue construction paper

Lesson 8: Creating and Writing About Patterns
- ☐ journal
- ☐ yarn
- ☐ thread

Final Project: Patterns Poster or Patterns Presentation
- ☐ 2 poster boards

Unit 2: Patterns in Sounds, Words, and Actions

Common Materials
- ☐ scissors
- ☐ glue
- ☐ construction paper
- ☐ colored pencils or crayons
- ☐ paper* (5.2 - Option 1)
- ☐ Music
- ☐ lined paper
- ☐ colored pencils or markers
- ☐ colored pencils or crayons* (5.2 - Option 2)
- ☐ simple picture books
- ☐ paper

Lesson 1: Word Patterns
- ☐ book of nursery rhymes
- ☐ paper and/or index cards* (1.3 - Option 2)

Lesson 2: Making Word Patterns
- ☐ rhyming picture books
- ☐ stapler
- ☐ ruler

Lesson 3: Poetry Patterns
- ☐ books of poetry for children

Lesson 4: Sentence Patterns
- ☐ blank paper

Lesson 5: Story Patterns
- ☐ simple storybook

Lesson 6: Sound Patterns
- ☐ glass
- ☐ musical instrument

Unit 2: Patterns in Sounds, Words, and Actions

☐ spoon

Lesson 7: Making Sound and Action Patterns
☐ variety of musical instruments

Final Project: Patterns Video
☐ device to play music

☐ video camera or digital camera that takes video

Unit 3: Patterns in Your World

Common Materials
☐ scissors

☐ crayons or colored pencils

☐ glue

☐ blank paper

☐ construction paper

☐ calendar

☐ laminated calendar

☐ markers

☐ tennis ball

☐ construction paper of different colors

☐ brass brads

Lesson 2: Patterns of Growth
☐ bean seeds or sunflower seeds

☐ clear plastic cup

☐ pictures of your child at different ages

☐ small rocks

☐ soil

Lesson 3: Night and Day
☐ basketball

☐ flashlight

☐ globe or basketball

☐ golf or ping-pong ball

☐ masking tape

Lesson 5: Calendar Patterns
☐ dry-erase marker

☐ glue or glue stick

☐ index cards

☐ lined paper

☐ poster board

Lesson 6: Seasonal Weather Patterns
☐ map of the United States

Lesson 7: Patterns at Home
☐ quilts with patterns

☐ thick and thin markers or pens

Lesson 8: Symmetrical Patterns
☐ paint or glue

Lesson 9: Counting Patterns
☐ paper clips, pennies, or counting bears

☐ pennies

Lesson 10: Tracing Patterns
☐ attribute blocks

☐ craft materials to decorate holiday cut-outs

☐ fabric, wood, or plastic

☐ markers, glitter, paint

☐ paintbrush

☐ stencil paint

☐ stencils or cardboard

© Copyright 2019 Epiphany Curriculum, LLC

Do not copy or distribute without written permission from Epiphany Curriculum, LLC.

Page 8

Unit 3: Patterns in Your World

Lesson 11: Patterns in Graphs

☐ block

☐ large bowl or small tub

☐ penny

☐ cotton ball

☐ leaf

☐ sponge

Final Project: Patterns All Around Lapbook

☐ fabric pieces

☐ manila filing folder

☐ magazines

* - Indicates a material that is either optional or may not be used.

Unit 1: Identifying and Creating Visual Patterns

This unit will help your child learn to identify many different types of patterns, including color, shape, and number. After identifying different types of patterns, he will learn to extend those patterns and predict what comes next. The final project includes creating a poster or a presentation to demonstrate the variety of patterns he has learned.

Vocabulary

Review vocabulary daily to achieve mastery.

word	definition
pattern	can be made of parts, shapes, or objects that repeat themselves in the same way over and over again
ABAB pattern	pattern made up of two parts that follow each other in the same order
AABB pattern	pattern made of two parts that work in pairs and repeat themselves in the same order to make a pattern
extend	to make something longer
ABC pattern	pattern made of three separate members/objects that repeat themselves in the same order

Unit Review Sheet

These facts and definitions should be mastered throughout this unit. This page can be used for periodic review and study as you are finishing the unit and in the future.

Lesson 1: What Is a Pattern?

- A **pattern** can be made of parts, shapes, or objects that repeat themselves in the same way over and over again.

Lesson 2: Recognizing Types of Patterns

- An **ABAB pattern** is made up of two parts that follow each other in the same order.
- An **AABB pattern** is made of two parts that work in pairs and repeat themselves in the same order to make a pattern.

Lesson 3: What Comes Next?

- **Extend** means to make something longer.
- To extend a pattern means to continue the pattern where it ends, making it longer.

Lesson 4: Extending a Pattern

- Patterns can be repeated over and over again.

Lesson 5: Making Color Patterns

- Patterns can be made using a variety of color combinations.

Lesson 6: Shapes and Patterns

- An **ABC pattern** has three separate members/objects that repeat themselves in the same order.

Lesson 7: Making Number Patterns

- Numbers and objects can be used to create patterns.

Lesson 8: Creating and Writing About Patterns

- To find a pattern, you have to look for the parts in the pattern and how the parts repeat themselves.

Lesson 1: What Is a Pattern? (2 Days)

Getting Started

? Questions to Explore

- How can patterns be made or found?
- What makes something a pattern?
- What strategies can be used for finding patterns?

📖 Facts and Definitions

- A **pattern** can be made of parts, shapes, or objects that repeat themselves in the same way over and over again.

⊙ Skills

- Identify patterns using knowledge of properties of objects (S)
- Name the ordinal positions in a sequence such as first, second, and third (M)
- Use words such as "before" or "after" to describe relative position in a sequence of events or objects (M)

✂ Materials

- ✓ *Busy Bugs: A Book About Patterns* by Jayne Harvey
- ✓ markers or crayons
- ✓ strips of red and blue construction paper
- ✓ Unifix cubes or Legos
- ✓ Caterpillar Patterns game
- ✓ scissors
- ✓ tape or glue

Introduction

Ask your child if she knows what a pattern is. Give her three strips of red paper and three strips of blue. (Unifix cubes or Legos would also work.) Ask her to organize the strips. If she groups them by color, talk about how to sort things according to similarities and differences. Explain that, in addition to sorting, we can also make patterns with objects.

Moving from left to right, start a red-blue-red-blue pattern using the strips of paper. Ask your child to continue the pattern by naming the color that will come next. Then ask her again what color strip she thinks should come next. Help her create her own pattern from the red and blue strips. Explain to her that a pattern can be made up of parts, shapes, or objects that repeat themselves in the same way over and over again.

Note: Patterns are one of the most important concepts young children can learn. A solid foundational understanding will equip children to excel in science and math. An understanding of patterns can also be helpful in spelling and reading mechanics.

If your child is familiar with the types of patterns covered in the lessons of this unit, provide opportunities for more challenging patterns. Some patterns you might want to include are AAABBCCC, ABBC, AABBBCC, and ABAABBAAABBB...

Activities

Activity 1: Busy Bugs

To introduce the concept of patterns, read the story, *Busy Bugs*, by Jayne Harvey. Look at the cover of the story and ask your child to identify the title and the author's name. Encourage your child to read the title and to guess what the story is about.

First, read the story aloud to your child, encouraging her to follow along. The second time, let your child attempt to read the story aloud. Provide assistance as needed.

Turn to pages 6-11 and ask your child what types of patterns she sees. Explain that patterns can be found in nature. For example, the spider's web follows a pattern. Different spiders create different types of patterns on their webs. Now look at pages 12-25 and explain that many patterns are made of parts that repeat themselves in the same way over and over again. Ask her to explain the patterns found on these pages.

Ask the following questions:

- Have you ever seen a pattern? Where?
- What are some places where patterns can be found?
- Have you ever made a pattern? If so, when?

Activity 2: Bug Patterns

Select one of the following options for your child to complete. The second option is more challenging than the first option.

Option 1

For this activity, give your child the two pages called "Bug Patterns" (Option 1). On the first page, she will find three rows of patterns. Ask her to describe the patterns that the bugs make in each row. She will then cut the pictures out from the second page and paste them in the blank spaces to complete the patterns on the first page. The caterpillar has stripes that follow a pattern, so the stripes can be drawn in. Finally, she can color the objects in the patterns once she has completed them.

On a separate sheet of paper, ask your child to draw some of her own bug patterns using spiders, ladybugs, butterflies. etc. The bugs on the page, "Drawing Bugs," can be used to guide her in drawing the bugs for her own patterns.

Option 2

On the first page of "Bug Patterns" (Option 2), your child will cut out the pictures of the bugs. Encourage her to arrange the bugs into different patterns, starting with two bugs and then working with three bugs. As she creates each pattern, ask her to name the objects in the pattern in order as they occur. For example, "butterfly, ant, butterfly, ant..."

Once your child begins using three different insects, encourage her to try using two or three of the same bugs in a row to make a pattern. If your child is ready, explain that each item in a pattern is assigned a letter. When the item repeats, the same letter is assigned to the item. (This will be covered in greater detail in Lesson 2.)

The second "Bug Patterns" page shows two caterpillars. On the first caterpillar, encourage your child to continue the pattern. On the second caterpillar, ask her to make up her own pattern on the caterpillar's back.

Activity 3: Caterpillar Patterns Game

To practice patterns with colors, open the Caterpillar Patterns game. Place the game pieces, color side up, in front of your child. There are eight Level 1 caterpillars that show color patterns. Rather than following the directions for the game at this point, lay out the Level 1 caterpillars with solid colors (not shapes) and have your child place the correct color segment on each body. Start with the AB patterns and then move to the more challenging ABC, AAB, and ABB patterns. Upon completing the patten, have your child explain each one.

Day 2

Activity 4: More Patterns

This activity has two options. Option 1 asks your child to describe the patterns she sees, and Option 2 asks her to create her own patterns. Choose an option for your child to complete.

Option 1: Do You See a Pattern?

To complete this activity, your child will describe the patterns on the sheet called "Do You See a Pattern?" Let her take a few moments to analyze each row and then explain the pattern she sees. Encourage her to use the following language to describe the pattern: "First, there is _____. Next, there is _____. Next, there is _____...." She should point to each item as she describes it. Then ask her to color/trace the objects so that their colors also follow a pattern. For example, she can trace the A's in red and the B's in blue.

Option 2: Can You Make a Pattern?

On the page, "Can You Make a Pattern?" (Option 2), cut out all of the objects and ask your child to design different patterns using the objects. Encourage her to group related objects together for her pattern sequences. Encourage her to think of as many ways as she can to organize her patterns and to explain each pattern she creates.

Activity 5: Is It a Pattern?

For this activity, your child will decide if each set of objects makes a pattern or not. She can write a "P" next to the sets that are patterns and "N" next to the sets that are not patterns. Ask her what could be done to make patterns on the rows that don't have them. Let her color the objects in the rows with patterns. There are two options for this activity; Option 2 contains more challenging patterns than Option 1.

Option 1

On the sheet called "Is It a Pattern?" (Option 1), your child will decide if each set of objects makes a pattern or not.

Option 2

The patterns on this option are more challenging than the first option. On the page, "Is it a Pattern?" (Option 2), your child will decide if each set of objects makes a pattern or not.

Activity 6: Playing the Caterpillar Patterns Game

Play the Caterpillar Patterns game using the color pattern bodies only. Follow the direction for Level 1 play.

Activity 7: Handwriting

Make a pattern and let your child write or copy three sentences to describe the pattern: *First, there is _____. Next there is _____. Then there is _____.*

Wrapping Up

Conclusion

Ask your child what a pattern is. Ask her to describe how she finds patterns in sets of objects.

Lesson 2: Recognizing Types of Patterns

Getting Started

? Questions to Explore

- How can patterns be made or found?
- What makes something a pattern?
- What are some ways to find patterns?

📖 Facts and Definitions

- An **ABAB pattern** is made up of two parts that follow each other in the same order.
- An **AABB pattern** is made of two parts that work in pairs and repeat themselves in the same order to make a pattern.

⊙ Skills

- Identify patterns using knowledge of properties of objects (S)
- Name the ordinal positions in a sequence such as first, second, and third (M)
- Use words such as "before" or "after" to describe relative position in a sequence of events or objects (M)

✂ Materials

- ✓ *Busy Bugs: A Book About Patterns* by Jayne Harvey
- ✓ Caterpillar Patterns game
- ✓ scissors
- ✓ beads or coins* (Activity 3 - optional)
- ✓ letters "A" and "B" cut out of paper
- ✓ strips of yellow and green construction paper

Introduction

Tell your child that there are different types of patterns. We can determine the types of patterns by looking at the number of objects in the set and how they repeat themselves. Cut out four letter A's and four letter B's and give them to your child. Tell him to make a pattern by having a B come after each A.

Now cut out same-sized strips of yellow and green paper (4 of each) and ask your child to use the strips and to make a yellow-green-yellow, etc. pattern. Ask him how many colors are in the set. Explain to him that, even though he is not using letters, he still has an ABAB pattern. Point out that the yellow is *A* and the green is *B*. Ask him to place a letter A beneath each yellow strip in the pattern and a letter B beneath each green strip in the pattern. Explain to him that he has demonstrated an ABAB pattern using yellow and green strips of paper.

Activities

Activity 1: An ABAB Pattern

Review the concept that when two objects repeat themselves in a pattern, it is called an **ABAB pattern**. An ABAB pattern does not mean you always have to use the letters A and B. It means that there are two objects in the pattern that follow each other.

Give your child the sheet called "An ABAB Pattern." For this activity, your child will identify the rows that are patterns. Then he will decide if each identified pattern is an ABAB pattern or not. Remind him that a pattern is made up of parts that repeat themselves in the same way, over and over again.

It may help for you to explain that each object is assigned a letter; next, show him how to label the objects, A and B, in each pattern. The first object is an A, the second a B, etc. There are boxes beneath the pictures where he can record the letters. First he will decide if the row follows a pattern. If it does, he needs to determine if it is an ABAB pattern.

Activity 2: What Is the Pattern? (ABAB or AABB)

Explain to your child that you are going to show him a set of letters and you want him to decide if the set is a pattern or not. He should explain how he decided. Put out two A's, followed by 2 B's, followed by 2 A's....

Ask him if the objects make a pattern and how many objects are in the pattern. Explain to him that this is an AABB pattern. In an **AABB pattern**, the objects that continue the pattern come in pairs/sets of two. There are still only two different objects used, but they appear in sets of two.

Give your child the yellow and green strips. Tell him to make an AABB pattern with the strips, starting with yellow. To check his answer, ask him to write a letter on each strip. "A" can be for the yellow strips and "B" can be the green strips.

Give your child the sheet called "What Is the Pattern?" On this sheet, he will decide if each pattern is an ABAB pattern or an AABB pattern. Encourage him to label the objects with A's and B's. The first row has been done for him.

Activity 3: Finding Patterns

Before beginning this activity, it might be helpful to introduce AAB and ABB patterns to your child using beads or other objects. You can also use three colors of beads or quarters, pennies, and dimes to introduce an ABC pattern. (The ABC pattern will be covered in detail in Lesson 6.)

For this activity, give your child the Level 1 caterpillars from the Caterpillar Patterns game. These are the caterpillars with solid colors. Ask him to describe the pattern of each caterpillar and to sort them into ABAB patterns, AAB patterns, ABB patterns, and ABC patterns. In the stack, you will find some caterpillars that are blank. On these caterpillars, have your child use the colored tiles to create an AABB pattern.

Activity 4: Handwriting

Let your child write or copy a sentence about the book, *Busy Bugs*.

Wrapping Up

Conclusion

Ask your child to explain to you the difference between an ABAB pattern and an AABB pattern. Ask him how he can decide if a pattern is ABAB or AABB. Reread the book, *Busy Bugs*, and ask your child to point out the ABAB and AABB patterns.

© Copyright 2019 Epiphany Curriculum, LLC

Do not copy or distribute without written permission from Epiphany Curriculum, LLC.

Page 16

Lesson 3: What Comes Next?

Getting Started

? Questions to Explore

- How can patterns be made or found?
- What types of patterns can be found?
- How can you find the order of a pattern?
- How can patterns be extended?

📖 Facts and Definitions

- **Extend** means to make something longer.
- To extend a pattern means to continue the pattern where it ends, making it longer.

⊙ Skills

- Predict what comes next in a pattern (M)
- Name the ordinal positions in a sequence such as first, second, and third (M)
- Use words such as "before" or "after" to describe relative position in a sequence of events or objects (M)

✂ Materials

- ✓ *Busy Bugs: A Book About Patterns* by Jayne Harvey
- ✓ glue
- ✓ squares cut out of two colors of construction paper
- ✓ black marker
- ✓ scissors
- ✓ Unifix cubes or Legos

Introduction

Ask your child to explain what it means for something to have a pattern. Remind her that patterns have an order that is repeated over and over. Cut 8 squares out of two colors of paper. (You can use Unifix cubes or Legos, if you prefer.) Form an ABAB pattern with four of the squares and show the pattern to your child. Ask her what would come next. Then ask her to explain how she knows what would come next. Review the concept that in order to know what comes next in a pattern, you have to identify the objects in the pattern and the order in which they repeat themselves.

When you **extend** something, you make it longer or continue it. Explain that when we add objects to a pattern, we call it extending the pattern. To extend a pattern, you have to identify the pattern, think about what should come next, and then add the appropriate objects.

Activities

Activity 1: Patterns Repeat

Choose an option for your child to complete. In Option 1, she will cut out objects and use them to extend existing patterns. In Option 2, she will form her own patterns in addition to extending existing patterns.

Option 1

Let your child cut out the objects on the page, "What Comes Next?" (Option 1). The objects are relatively small, so she may need help cutting. Show your child the page called "Patterns Repeat" (Option 1 & 2 - Page 1). She can analyze each row of patterns. As she is looking at each row, ask her the following questions:

- What comes first in the pattern? Next?
- What comes before _____?
- What comes after _____?

Now ask her to identify each pattern as an ABAB, AABB, or ABC pattern by writing it in the "Type" column. She can then glue the cut-out objects to extend each pattern.

After your child has extended the pattern, she can label each object she added to the pattern with an A, B, or C.

Option 2

Show your child the page called "Patterns Repeat" (Option 2 - Page 2). Encourage your child to cut out the pictures, which she will use to form patterns. After she has cut out the objects, place 2 objects in front of her and ask her to begin an ABAB pattern starting with the two objects you set out; she will use other cut-out pictures to complete the pattern. Likewise, put out three objects and ask her to make an ABC pattern and then give her two objects and ask her to begin an AABB pattern. She will again use the cut-out pictures to complete and/or extend the pattern.

As she completes each pattern, ask the following questions:

- What comes first in the pattern? Next?
- What comes before _____?
- What comes after _____?

Using the "Patterns Repeat" (Option 1 & 2 - Page 1) page, ask your child to identify the pattern as an ABAB, AABB, or ABC pattern. She can then draw an object in each blank to extend each pattern. After your child has extended the pattern, she can identify and label the new items she added to the pattern with an A, B, or C.

Activity 2: A Different Kind of Pattern

Before you begin this activity, be sure that your child understands the concept of thick and thin. You will be using the words "thick" and "thin" to describe the shapes in the pattern. You can review the concept of thick and thin by examining the thickness of a variety of books.

For this activity, your child will be looking at patterns that extend in all directions (radiating patterns), not rows of objects that form patterns. Look at both pictures on the page, "A Different Kind of Pattern," and ask her the following questions:

Picture 1:

- Describe the center square. Are the lines that form the square thick or thin?
- Describe the square that surrounds the center circle.
- Describe the square that comes next.
- Do you see a pattern?
- What type of square would you add to the outside square?
- Can you draw a new square on the outside? Would it be better to use a pencil or a marker? (Show your child the difference between a pencil line and a marker line.)

<u>Picture 2</u>:

- Describe the center circle. Is it thick or thin?
- Describe the circle that surrounds the center circle.
- Describe the circle that comes next.
- Do you see a pattern?
- What type of circle would you add around the outside circle?
- Can you draw a new circle on the outside? Would it be better to use a pencil or a marker?

Now on a separate sheet of paper, ask your child to draw a similar pattern using a triangle as her shape. To extend this activity, she can use different shapes and even add different colors to her radiating pattern.

Activity 3: Bug Patterns
Ask your child to identify the ABAB, AABB, and ABC patterns in *Busy Bugs*. Let her illustrate what would come next if the patterns were to continue.

Activity 4: Handwriting
Let your child write or copy a sentence that asks a question about what comes next in a pattern: *What do you see after the* _____? Review the fact that sentences that ask questions end in question marks.

Wrapping Up

Conclusion
Ask your child what it means to extend a pattern. Ask her to describe how she knows what comes next in a pattern. Ask your child if a pattern is always a row of items. Ask her to describe a different type of pattern.

What Comes Next?
www.movingbeyondthepage.com/link/556
At this link, your child can play the Pattern Mania game online.
http://www.primarygames.com/patterns/start.htm

© Copyright 2019 Epiphany Curriculum, LLC

Do not copy or distribute without written permission from Epiphany Curriculum, LLC.

Page 19

Lesson 4: Extending a Pattern

Getting Started

? Questions to Explore

- How can patterns be made or found?
- How do you extend a pattern?

📖 Facts and Definitions

- Patterns can be repeated over and over again.

⊙ Skills

- Predict what comes next in a pattern (M)
- Name the ordinal positions in a sequence such as first, second, and third (M)

✂ Materials

- ✓ crayons, markers, colored pencils
- ✓ green construction paper
- ✓ paper clips
- ✓ red construction paper
- ✓ forks and spoons
- ✓ Legos
- ✓ pennies and nickels
- ✓ Scissors

Introduction

Explore the idea that a pattern can continue as long as you repeat the order of its items.

Activities

Activity 1: Extending a Pattern

Explain to your child that sometimes patterns do not repeat themselves but grow as they continue. Cut out 15 red squares and 15 green circles from construction paper.

Lay down 1 square and 1 circle, and then lay down two squares and two circles. Ask your child what would come next. If he does not guess 3 squares followed by 3 circles, place the shapes in the row, and then see if he can guess what comes next.

See if your child can continue a similar pattern using 2 colors of Legos (the same size) or a penny and nickel for the objects in his pattern.

Activity 2: Writing About a Pattern

In this activity, your child will gather materials, read the pattern listed (or you can read the pattern to him), and then recreate and extend the pattern. Next, he will answer questions about each pattern. There are two options for this activity; Option 1 provides more guidance with the questions. Decide which option your child will complete. Note: This activity contains the new pattern ABBA. You can either model the pattern for him beforehand using beads or other items or let him try to figure out the pattern on his own.

Option 1

For this option, your child will gather the objects used on the "Writing About a Pattern" (Option 1) sheet and recreate each pattern. After that, he will extend the pattern, repeating it two more times. Next, he will complete the sentence about the given pattern by circling the correct answer. Let him determine whether each pattern is an ABAB, AABB, or ABBA. Ask your child to select his own sets of objects to create two more unique patterns and to decide if his new patterns are ABAB, AABB, or ABBA.

Option 2 (Advanced)

For this activity, use the "Writing About a Pattern" (Option 2) sheet. Your child will read the words for each pattern, gather the objects, and create the given pattern. Then he will extend the pattern, repeating it two more times. Next he will complete the sentence about the given pattern. Let him determine whether each pattern is an ABAB, AABB, or ABBA. Ask him to select his own sets of objects to create two more unique patterns and to decide if his new patterns are ABAB, AABB, or ABBA patterns. To extend this activity, let him write the names of the objects he used for patterns on a separate sheet of paper.

Activity 3: Object Patterns

For this activity, create a variety of patterns with real objects for your child to extend.

Activity 4: Handwriting

Let your child copy or write a sentence about a pattern he made today.

Wrapping Up

Conclusion

Review the idea that the parts that make up patterns repeat themselves again and again. Ask your child to explain how he extends a pattern.

Lesson 5: Making Color Patterns

Getting Started

? Questions to Explore

- How do you make a pattern?
- What kinds of patterns can be made?
- What materials can be used to make patterns?

📖 Facts and Definitions

- Patterns can be made using a variety of color combinations.

⊙ Skills

- Create patterns using knowledge of properties of objects (S)
- Compare attributes of two objects using appropriate vocabulary (M)
- Use words that describe color, size, and location (LA)

✂ Materials

- ✓ cookie sheet
- ✓ green construction paper
- ✓ paper towels
- ✓ Scissors
- ✓ tape* (Activity 2 - optional)
- ✓ Zip-lock bags

- ✓ food coloring
- ✓ large macaroni
- ✓ rubbing alcohol
- ✓ solid colored dot/circle stickers
- ✓ yarn or twine

Introduction

Ask your child if she can think of ways to use colors to create patterns. Let her demonstrate her ideas. Show her examples of patterns that use color combinations, like in fabric or jewelry. Explain that many patterns are created using different colors that repeat themselves in the same order.

Activities

Activity 1: Caterpillars on Leaves Pattern

Give your child a piece of green construction paper. She can cut out the leaves on the "Caterpillar Leaf Patterns" sheet and then trace them on green construction paper, making three or four leaves. Discuss how the leaf is a pattern that she is tracing, so she can make more identical leaves.

Now provide her with some colored dot/circle stickers. Explain that you want her to make caterpillars out of the circle stickers and put them on the leaves. Each caterpillar she makes should follow a color pattern.

Do the first one with your child so you can model the idea. You can alternate two or three colors of stickers to create a caterpillar pattern. Let her complete three more caterpillars on the leaves. Ask her to describe the patterns she creates. She can make ABAB, AABB, ABBA, or any other pattern she comes up with. If your child has an advanced understanding of patterns, encourage her to create more complex patterns and then to describe them.

On a separate sheet of paper, let your child use the color word (or the first letter of the color word) to show the pattern with words or letters. For example, if one of her caterpillars follows a yellow-red-yellow-red pattern, she could write out the words or Y, R, Y, R.

Activity 2: Necklace Patterns

For this activity, your child will create colored bead necklaces or bracelets using macaroni. First, you will dye the macaroni (refer to the directions that follow), and then your child will thread the macaroni onto pieces of yarn to make beaded jewelry. Explain to your child that each necklace must follow a pattern. Let her create ABAB and AABB patterned necklaces. If she is ready for more advanced patterns, she can create necklaces with an ABC pattern or any other more challenging pattern she can think of.

NOTE: Wrapping some tape at the end of the yarn will help your child thread the yarn through the macaroni. Twine may also work if she has problems with the yarn.

Directions for making colored macaroni:

1. Mix 2 Tbsp. rubbing alcohol and 3 or 4 drops of food coloring in a small container. Set aside.
2. Pour 1 cup uncooked macaroni noodles into a large bag with a zipper seal.
3. Add the colored rubbing alcohol to the bag.
4. Zip the bag closed.
5. Squeeze the bag gently with your hands for 1 or 2 minutes until the macaroni noodles are evenly colored.
6. Cover a cookie sheet with paper towels.
7. Pour the macaroni out of the bag onto the cookie sheet. Spread out the noodles and let them dry.
8. Store colored macaroni in plastic containers with lids.
9. Follow the same directions using different colors of food coloring for a variety of colors of macaroni.

Note: To extend this activity, your child can create necklaces for friends and family members, practicing a variety of patterns.

Activity 3: Handwriting

Let your child write or copy a sentence that describes something she created today.

Wrapping Up

Conclusion

Let your child demonstrate a variety of color patterns using blocks, counting bears, colored shapes, etc.

Lesson 6: Shapes and Patterns (2 Days)

Getting Started

? Questions to Explore

- How can patterns be made or found?
- How can numbers, shapes, and words form patterns?

📖 Facts and Definitions

- An **ABC pattern** has three separate members/objects that repeat themselves in the same order.

⊙ Skills

- Identify patterns using knowledge of properties of objects (S)
- Name the ordinal positions in a sequence such as first, second, and third (M)

✂ Materials

- ✓ attribute blocks
- ✓ glue or tape
- ✓ markers or crayons
- ✓ Scissors
- ✓ Caterpillar Patterns game
- ✓ lined paper
- ✓ red, yellow, and blue construction paper
- ✓ thick paper or foam

Introduction

Give your child the set of attribute blocks. Tell him to practice making patterns with the shapes. Give him time to explore and explain his patterns. If you do not have attribute blocks, cut out large and small circles, squares, and triangles in three different colors. All the large shapes should be about three inches in height and the small shapes about 1½ inches in height. Save these shapes to use for future activities in Unit 2.

Review the ABAB and AABB patterns with the shapes. Make a pattern with three different shapes and explain that when you add a third object, you give it the letter C. Patterns with three different objects in a row that repeat themselves in the same order are called ABC patterns. Ask your child to show you an ABC pattern with the attribute blocks.

Activities

Activity 1: Shapes and Patterns

For the activity, your child will use the attribute blocks to recreate each set of shapes on the "Shapes and Patterns" sheets. These pages will need to be glued or taped together to make longer rows for the patterns. Ask your child to describe the order of the shapes in the sets. For example, he might say, "The first shape is a small circle. The second shape is a small square. The third shape is a small circle. The fourth shape is a small square. The fifth shape is a...."

He will then decide if each set of shapes is a pattern or not. If it is a pattern, he can then describe the pattern saying, "Circle, Square, Circle, Square...."

Finally, he can take off the blocks and label the shapes with A, B, or C (inside each shape) and tell you whether the set of shapes is an ABAB, an AABB, or an ABC pattern.

Activity 2: Reading Patterns

In this activity, your child will follow written patterns. Choose an option for your child to complete — Option 2 is more advanced.

Option 1

Give your child all of the large triangles, squares, and circles (either attribute blocks or shapes you cut out). On the "Reading Patterns" (Option 1) sheets, your child will circle the beginning letter of each word in the pattern. Then he will sound out each word and create each pattern with his attribute blocks. For the longer rows, you can cut off the bottom row and glue it to the end of the previous row to make one continuous pattern. Finally, he will describe the patterns as ABAB, AABB, or ABC.

Encourage him to make an ABC pattern from colors instead of shapes, using the attribute blocks: red, yellow, blue, red, yellow, blue...

Ask him to make an ABAB pattern using color, not shape, as the attribute.

Option 2 (Advanced)

For this activity, which uses the "Reading Patterns" (Option 2) sheets, your child will read the words that describe the pattern and then create the pattern with the attribute blocks or cut-out shapes. Explain to him that his pattern must be created by the shapes listed, but it must also follow a color pattern at the same time. This activity is much more challenging because the child must consider two attributes in his patterns — color and shape. If you do not have enough shapes in the same color to complete a pattern, your child can trace the shapes onto construction paper and cut them out. For the longer rows, you can cut off the bottom row and glue it to the end of the previous row so the shapes all fit on one line.

As your child designs each pattern, he can describe the pattern as ABAB, AABB, or ABC.

To extend this activity and make it even more challenging, your child can add the thickness of the shape to the pattern instead of color. He may need to cut shapes from thick paper or, even better, foam if he does not have enough of a certain shape to make the pattern.

Activity 3: Handwriting

Let your child write or copy a sentence about a pattern he found today.

Day 2

Activity 4: Creeping Caterpillar Shape Patterns

Locate the bodies that have shapes in the Caterpillar Patterns game. Play Level 2 of the game.

When you are finished, give your child the caterpillars with shapes from the Caterpillar Patterns game and ask him to describe the pattern of each caterpillar, sorting them into ABAB patterns, AAB patterns, ABB patterns, and ABC patterns. In the stack, you will find some caterpillars that are blank. On these caterpillars, have your child use the shape tiles to create an AABB pattern.

Activity 5: The Shape of Things

Gather a variety of objects that are the same shape. Create patterns with them and ask your child to identify the patterns. He may be confused because the objects are not identical, but he should begin to see what they have in common.

For example: circle, rectangle, circle, rectangle. This pattern could be represented with any of the following objects: round clock, book, plate, pillow, rubber band, and TV remote.

Wrapping Up

Conclusion

Ask your child to make an ABAB pattern of his choice with his shapes. He can trace the shapes onto a separate sheet of paper and then color them. Follow this with an AABB pattern and an ABC pattern.

Shape Patterns Game
www.movingbeyondthepage.com/link/7892
At this website, you will find an advanced pattern game that you can provide if your child needs an extra level of challenge. NOTE: The games on this site are free to play on computers (PCs/Macs) but require a paid subscription to play on mobile devices.
https://www.abcya.com/games/shape_patterns

Words to Practice

On a sheet of lined paper, let your child practice writing the words *shape*, *color*, and *size*. Model writing each word for him.

Lesson 7: Making Number Patterns

Getting Started

? **Questions to Explore**

- How do you make a pattern?
- What kinds of patterns can be made?
- What materials can be used to make patterns?

📖 **Facts and Definitions**

- Numbers and objects can be used to create patterns.

⊙ **Skills**

- Create and extend patterns with actions, words, sound, and objects (M)
- Create patterns using knowledge of properties of objects (S)
- Identify and draw shapes (M)

✂ **Materials**

- ✓ counting bears or small items such as Legos,   ✓ Scissors
  pennies, paper clips, or beads

Introduction

Ask your child to demonstrate or explain ways numbers can be used to make patterns.

Activities

Activity 1: Creating Number Patterns

On the sheet, "Creating Number Patterns," your child will create patterns using numbers. She must include each number listed on the row to create ABAB, ABC, or AABB patterns. If your child needs help, do the first pattern together.

Activity 2: Number Patterns

For this activity, your child will create three patterns by writing numbers on the "Number Patterns" sheet. Remind her that patterns have parts that repeat in the same way. They can work with any one-digit numbers they choose. If you have a child who needs more challenge allow him to use two-digit numbers for the patterns. They can make ABB, AABB, ABC, ABB, or ABAB pattern combinations with the numbers they choose. If your child comes up with a new pattern for the numbers that is logical encourage him to identify the new pattern with letters - i.e. ABBC or AABBCC.

Activity 3: Number/Object Patterns

Use real objects to create a pattern. Ask your child to look at the pattern and write the numbers to represent the pattern. Cut out small squares of paper for her to record the numbers 1-5.

Example: Make a pattern using the following objects and quantities: 2 markers, 3 paperclips, 2 markers, 3 paperclips... Then your child can label the different quantities with her number cards: 2,3,2,3...

You can repeat this activity, creating new number patterns with different quantities and objects. Encourage your child to make her own patterns from the objects and to identify the number pattern of each set of objects. To add an extra level of challenge to this activity, encourage your child to increase the quantity of the objects used and the complexity of the patterns.

Wrapping Up

Conclusion
Review the idea that patterns can be made by numbers or objects.

© Copyright 2019 Epiphany Curriculum, LLC

Do not copy or distribute without written permission from Epiphany Curriculum, LLC.

Page 28

Lesson 8: Creating and Writing About Patterns (2 Days)

Getting Started

? Questions to Explore

- What are some strategies for finding patterns?
- How can patterns be made or found?
- Where can we find patterns?
- What are examples of patterns that can be made and/or found?

📖 Facts and Definitions

- To find a pattern, you have to look for the parts in the pattern and how the parts repeat themselves.

⊙ Skills

- Identify patterns using knowledge of properties of objects (S)
- Name the ordinal positions in a sequence such as first, second, and third (M)
- Use words such as "before" or "after" to describe relative position in a sequence of events or objects (M)

✂ Materials

- ✓ Caterpillar Patterns game
- ✓ lined paper
- ✓ materials to make a variety of patterns
- ✓ yarn
- ✓ journal
- ✓ markers or crayons
- ✓ thread

Introduction

Ask your child to think about different patterns and how he can determine their order. Review the idea that to describe a pattern, you have to figure out what parts make up the pattern and how those parts repeat. You can decide what comes first, second, and third, and then think about what comes before and after.

Activities

Activity 1: Writing About Patterns

Use the activity sheets, "Creating and Writing about a Pattern" (Option 1 or 2) to complete one of the following options.

Option 1

This option is best for children who are not strong writers or need visual cues to aid reading. Ask your child to create an example of each type of pattern using the words on the list. He can attempt to copy the words or the first letter of each word. Next, he can illustrate the words to form patterns with pictures. Finally, ask him to describe each pattern.

Option 2 (Advanced)

This option is best for children with stronger reading and writing skills. Ask your child to create an example of each type of pattern by using object words on the list. Next, he can illustrate the objects that create the pattern. Finally, ask him to complete the words at the beginning of each line — First, Then, Next comes...

Activity 2: Pattern Race

For this activity, call out the letters for a pattern (ABAB, AABB, or ABC) and see how quickly your child can recreate the patterns in a drawing or with objects. They can use logos, beads, coins, pattern blocks, or any other types of duplicate manipulatives to create the patterns. They can draw objects on paper to represent the patterns if they so choose.

Activity 3: Sequence Words

Encourage your child to brainstorm words that describe the order in which things occur. Record these on a sheet of lined paper. Then he can write the following words five times in his journal: *first, then,* and *next.*

Day 2

Activity 4: Guess the Pattern

This is a game that you can play with your child. Let your child collect a variety of objects (blocks, paper clips, pencils, bear counters, stuffed animals), anything that allows you to repeat. You will create a pattern with some of the objects, and your child will figure out the pattern and describe it. Include shape patterns, object patterns, and color patterns. You can make patterns that continue all directions by using thread and yarn. Make a circle (or another shape) with the thread and then a larger circle around it with the yarn and continue the pattern from there. You can also ask your child to identify the patterns as ABAB, ABC, AABB, AAB, etc. To extend this activity, let your child create his own patterns.

Activity 5: Describe the Pattern

For this activity, repeat a pattern from Activity 4 that your child was able to guess. You can let him choose his favorite pattern. Ask him to describe the pattern using the activity sheet, "Describe the Pattern." (If the pattern he selects has only two objects, mark out the line before "and" on the second line of the sentence at the top of the page.) If he is not able to write words, assign a letter to each item. Make sure that each pattern includes a minimum of eight items. The last sentence describes the pattern as a color, number, shape, or object pattern.

To extend this activity, use patterns created in Activity 1.

Activity 6: Creeping Caterpillars (Build Your Own)

Play Level 3 of the Caterpillar Patterns game. This is the most challenging level of the game because children build their own color or shape patterns.

Activity 7: Handwriting

Let your child write or copy two or three sentences that describe a pattern he made today.

Wrapping Up

Conclusion

Ask your child to describe the different kinds of patterns that can be made and how he can find patterns.

Final Project: Patterns Poster or Patterns Presentation

Getting Started

? **Questions to Explore**

- What kinds of patterns can be made?
- How do you make a pattern?
- What materials can be used to make patterns?

⊙ **Skills**

- Create and extend patterns with actions, words, sound, and objects (M)
- Create patterns using knowledge of properties of objects (S)
- Sequence events (M)
- Produce rhyming words (LA)

✂ **Materials**

- ✓ 2 poster boards
- ✓ materials to make a variety of patterns
- ✓ glue or tape

Introduction

Explain to your child that she will complete a final project on making patterns. She will choose whether she wants to create a poster or do a presentation. Through the project, she will demonstrate her understanding of the different types of patterns that can be made. Let her decide which project sounds most interesting.

Activities

Pattern Project

The following seven patterns must be featured on the poster board or in the presentation:

- Color Pattern
- Shape Pattern
- Object Pattern
- ABAB Pattern
- ABC Pattern
- AABB Pattern
- Number Pattern

Option 1: Poster Board

Write the patterns described above on a piece of paper and discuss each one. Let your child decide what materials she will use to display each pattern. The materials must be glued to poster board. For example, she might show a color pattern with beads, buttons, or sequins and a number pattern with pieces of construction paper or number stickers. Beside the name of each type of pattern, record the materials that will be used.

Take two poster boards and divide one into three sections and the other into four. Let your child label each section with the type of pattern and then let her create the patterns with materials that she can stick to the poster board. Provide assistance as needed. Hang her poster board up so that friends and family can read about the patterns she has been studying.

© Copyright 2019 Epiphany Curriculum, LLC

Page 31

Do not copy or distribute without written permission from Epiphany Curriculum, LLC.

<u>Option 2: Presentation</u>

If your child chooses to do a presentation on patterns, she will demonstrate the seven types of patterns from the list for an audience. On the sheets called "Script for Presentation," she can record the words she will use in her presentation. She will describe each pattern and then demonstrate an example of each pattern with a variety of materials. She will need to decide what materials she will use and then practice making the patterns.

Once she has prepared her presentation and practiced so that she knows exactly what she will say, she can make her presentation to friends or family.

Wrapping Up

Conclusion

After your child has completed her project, ask the following questions:

- How did you think your project went?
- What did you do well for your project?
- What do you think you could have done better?
- Which pattern did you enjoy creating most? Why?
- Which pattern was hardest to create? Why?
- What do you think people who saw your project learned about patterns?

© Copyright 2019 Epiphany Curriculum, LLC

Do not copy or distribute without written permission from Epiphany Curriculum, LLC.

Page 32

Unit 2: Patterns in Sounds, Words, and Actions

In this unit, your child will learn to create and extend patterns with objects, use words that describe patterns, and identify the order of events. Her final project will be a presentation of four different kinds of patterns that she will perform for her family and friends.

Vocabulary

Review vocabulary daily to achieve mastery.

word	definition
nouns	naming words that are for people, places, and things
verbs	action words that show what a person or thing is doing
rhyming words	words that follow the same pattern, also called rhythms
poem	a group of words that an author puts together to describe an object or situation that often helps the reader form a picture in her mind
naming words	nouns, or the name of people, places, and things
action words	verbs, or the word that describes what a person or thing is
sentences	a set of words that include a subject and predicate, begin with a capital letter, and usually end with a period

Unit Review Sheet

These facts and definitions should be mastered throughout this unit. This page can be used for periodic review and study as you are finishing the unit and in the future.

Lesson 1: Word Patterns

- Words that follow the same pattern are called **rhyming words**.

Lesson 2: Making Word Patterns

- Words that **rhyme** sound the same.
- Words that follow the same pattern are in the same word families.
- Words in the same word family are rhyming words.

Lesson 3: Poetry Patterns

- A **poem** is a group of words that an author puts together to describe an object or situation, and it often helps readers form a picture in their mind.
- A poem often contains words that follow the same pattern (rhyming words).

Lesson 4: Sentence Patterns

- Sentences follow patterns.
- **Naming words** are for people, places, and things. We call these words **nouns**.
- **Action words** describe what a person or thing is doing. We call these words **verbs**.
- **Sentences** begin with a capital letter and end with punctuation, such as a period.
- Some sentences follow the pattern of a person, place, or thing word (naming word) followed by an action word.

Lesson 5: Story Patterns

- Stories have a beginning, middle, and end.

Lesson 6: Sound Patterns

- Sounds can form patterns.
- We often call sound patterns **rhythms**.

Lesson 7: Making Sound and Action Patterns

- Different sounds can be combined to form patterns.

Lesson 1: Word Patterns

Getting Started

? Questions to Explore

- How can patterns be made or found?
- What makes something a pattern?

📖 Facts and Definitions

- Words that follow the same pattern are called **rhyming words**.

⊙ Skills

- Identify patterns using knowledge of properties of objects (S)
- Sort and classify objects (S and M)
- Use author's model of language (LA)
- Recognize that spoken language has identifiable speech sounds (LA)
- Understand that some words begin and end alike (LA)
- Become familiar with a variety of types of books: nursery rhymes, story books, and informational books (LA)

✂ Materials

- ✓ *Bear Hugs* by Karma Wilson and Suzanne Watts
- ✓ colored pencils or markers
- ✓ paper and/or index cards* (Activity 3 - Option 2)
- ✓ book of nursery rhymes
- ✓ lined paper
- ✓ scissors

Introduction

Say the following words to your child and ask her what she hears: *take, bake, rake*. Tell her that words can follow patterns. Explain that the three words that you just said follow a pattern; they all end with -ake. Explain that words that follow the same pattern are called rhyming words. Ask her if she can think of any other -ake words.

Activities

Activity 1: Word Patterns

Select one of the following options for your child to complete.

Option 1

Using the activity sheet called "Word Patterns" (Option 1), show your child the list of words in each row. Remind her that we can find patterns among words. Ask her if she sees a pattern among each set of words. Tell her to circle the part of the word that repeats. At the end, ask her to add another word that follows the same pattern. As an added challenge, she can also illustrate her word.

Option 2

Using the activity sheet called "Word Patterns" (Option 2), ask your child to label the items in each row. Explain that the words should follow the same pattern (rhyme). Ask her if she can identify words that will follow the same pattern. Tell her to label the pictures on the lines provided and to circle the part of the word that repeats. At the end, ask her to add another word that follows the same pattern. As an added challenge, she can also illustrate her word.

© Copyright 2019 Epiphany Curriculum, LLC

Do not copy or distribute without written permission from Epiphany Curriculum, LLC.

Page 35

Activity 2: Nursery Rhymes

Discuss the difference between a nursery rhyme and a storybook. A storybook follows the pattern of having a beginning, middle, and end. Nursery rhyme books are made up of many nursery rhymes, and within each rhyme are words that follow the same pattern — rhyming words.

Read a variety of nursery rhymes and let your child identify the rhyming words in each one. Encourage her to record the rhyming words she hears in each nursery rhyme on a sheet of lined paper. Ask your child to pick her favorite nursery rhyme. Then ask her to act out or illustrate the nursery rhyme.

Explain that some words in nursery rhymes sound the same but are not spelled the same. Explain that these words still rhyme. Many words that sound the same are not necessarily spelled the same. Write examples such as *wait/date, paid/fade,* and *mean/seen.*

Activity 3: Bear Hugs

Explain to your child that poetry is a form of writing that often uses words that follow the same sound pattern or rhyming words. Explain that poems are shorter than stories and usually describe an object or situation using descriptive language. Review that many rhyming words follow the same pattern, but words can rhyme that have different spelling patterns. For example, *pear/stare* and *blue/too* are pairs of rhyming words that do not follow the same spelling pattern. Read the poems in the book, *Bear Hugs,* to your child.

Next, choose an option for your child to complete.

Option 1

Have your child cut apart the list of illustrated words on the "Bear Hugs" (Option 1) word list sheet. Ask her to match the words that follow the same pattern, and then ask her if she can think of any other rhyming words that would fit with each pair. Encourage her to say each pair of words aloud and then add her new rhyming word to the pair.

Option 2 (Advanced)

Your child can cut apart the list of words on the "Bear Hugs" (Option 2) word list sheet. Then ask her to match the words that follow the same pattern (rhyming words). The words for this option are not illustrated. Ask her if she can think of any other words that would fit with each pair. Let her write each pair of words along with her new words on a separate piece of paper.

Note:

To extend this activity, let her identify examples of rhyming words that follow the same spelling pattern and others that do not. Encourage her to record rhyming words from the text, to cut them out, and to sort them into groups.

And/Or

To make this activity even more challenging, your child can identify five pairs of rhyming words in the text that follow the same spelling pattern and two pairs of words that rhyme but have different spelling patterns. She can record the words on a sheet of paper or on index cards (a rhyming word on each side).

Activity 4: Animals and Habitats

For this activity, reread the *Bear Hugs* story or encourage your child to read it, then let your child copy or dictate the names of the animals from the text. Ask her to identify the habitat where each animal lives. She can cut out the animal names and sort them into groups according to the habitats in which they live.

Note: To extend this activity, your child can make habitat pictures and draw the animals from the book in the picture.

Activity 5: Handwriting
Let your child write or copy a sentence using two rhyming words from *Bear Hugs*.

Wrapping Up

Conclusion
Ask your child what we call words that follow the same ending sound pattern but start with different letters (rhyming words). Say each of the following words and ask her to tell you rhyming words that follow the same pattern as each word: *hat, book, and play*.

Life Application
As you read stories with your child, encourage her to identify the rhyming words and the patterns she sees and hears.

Lesson 2: Making Word Patterns

Getting Started

? **Questions to Explore**

- How do you make a pattern?
- What kinds of patterns can be made?

📖 **Facts and Definitions**

- Words that **rhyme** sound the same.
- Words that follow the same pattern are in the same word families.
- Words in the same word family are rhyming words.

⊙ **Skills**

- Create and extend patterns with actions, words, sound, and objects (M)
- Create patterns using knowledge of properties of objects (S)
- Understand that letter combinations make words (LA)
- Recognize that the sequence of letters represents the sequence of sounds in a word (LA)
- Identify rhyming words (LA)

✂ **Materials**

- ✓ colored pencils or markers
- ✓ glue
- ✓ ruler
- ✓ stapler
- ✓ construction paper
- ✓ rhyming picture books
- ✓ scissors

Introduction

Ask your child what it means when we say that two words rhyme. Ask him to name pairs or sets of rhyming words. If he needs ideas, provide him with a word and let him think of a word(s) that rhymes with it.

Remind him that rhyming words are words that sound the same. Rhyming words follow the same letter pattern. Words that follow the same letter pattern are in the same word family, and these words rhyme with one another. For example, *pig, dig,* and *wig* are rhyming words that follow the same pattern and are in the same word family.

Activities

Activity 1: It's Time to Rhyme

Fold the sheet, "It's Time to Rhyme," in half vertically so that your child cannot see the illustrations. Your child will complete each sentence with a word that follows the same pattern as the underlined rhyming word. To check his answers, unfold the sheet and let him read each sentence.

He can then cut the sentences and illustrations apart and make a book of rhyming sentences. First, he can fold two pieces of construction paper in half for the pages, and then he can glue a sentence and an illustration on each page. Staple the book along the binding edge and let him put a title on the book, "It's Time to Rhyme." Then he can name himself as the author.

On the last two pages of the book, he can come up with two of his own sentences that contain rhyming words. Provide assistance as needed to help him record the sentences, but let him think of his own sentences.

© Copyright 2019 Epiphany Curriculum, LLC

Do not copy or distribute without written permission from Epiphany Curriculum, LLC.

Page 38

Activity 2: Word Patterns

Option 1

In this activity, your child is going to find words that follow the same pattern. Let your child look at the list of words on the "Word Patterns" (Option 1) sheet, and attempt to read each word. He can cut the words apart and sort the words that follow the same pattern. Explain that he is putting the words into word families.

Cut out four 4x6 inch rectangles from colored construction paper. Once your child has all the words sorted, he can identify the pattern and paste the word families on the pieces of construction paper. Each group of words can be labeled to identify the family. For example, the words *run, fun, sun*, and *bun* will be pasted together with the label "-un words" written at the top of the paper.

He can use these words to practice reading words in the same word family. You can also make new cards with words in other word families: -en, -ait, -et, -an, etc.

Option 2 (Advanced)

In this activity, your child will create words that follow the same pattern. Have him look at the first list of words on the "Word Patterns" (Option 2) sheet and ask him if he sees a pattern. Let him complete the pattern in List 1. For the next two lists, ask your child to create a list of words that follow the same pattern as the first word. If he needs guidance, give him a sheet with the letters of the alphabet and let him try different beginning letters that might complete the pattern to make words. Explain to him that he will put the words into word families. Next, let him cut the words apart.

Cut out four 4x6 inch rectangles from colored construction paper. Once your child has all the words cut apart and sorted, he can identify the pattern and then paste the word families on the pieces of construction paper. Each group of words can be given a label to identify the family. For example, the words *hit, kit, wit*, and *sit* can be pasted on together with the label "-it words."

He can use these words to practice reading words in the same word family. You can also make new cards with words in other word families - en, ait, et, an, etc.

Activity 3: Word Patterns in Books

Give your child a variety of picture books that rhyme. Help him to identify and record words from the text that have the same sound pattern (rhyme). Identify groups of words that follow the same spelling patterns and groups of rhyming words that do not follow the same spelling pattern.

Activity 4: Handwriting

Ask your child to write or copy a sentence that has two rhyming words.

Wrapping Up

Conclusion

Ask your child to explain how groups of words can follow a pattern. Ask him to name sets of words that are in the same word family.

Life Application

As your child is reading books, encourage him to identify any word patterns he finds. You can also make a poster for the wall and, as your child encounters words that are in the same word family, he can put them on the poster.

© Copyright 2019 Epiphany Curriculum, LLC

Do not copy or distribute without written permission from Epiphany Curriculum, LLC.

Page 39

Lesson 3: Poetry Patterns

Getting Started

? **Questions to Explore**

- How can patterns be made or found?
- What makes something a pattern?

📖 **Facts and Definitions**

- A **poem** is a group of words that an author puts together to describe an object or situation, and it often helps readers form a picture in their mind.
- A poem often contains words that follow the same pattern (rhyming words).

⊙ **Skills**

- Identify patterns using knowledge of properties of objects (S)
- Understand that some words begin and end alike (LA)
- Discuss, illustrate, or dramatize a story or poem (LA)
- Read or attempt to read simple text (LA)

✂ **Materials**

- ✓ *Bear Hugs* by Karma Wilson and Suzanne Watts   ✓ books of poetry for children
- ✓ colored pencils or crayons

Introduction

Tell your child that a poem has words that an author puts together to describe an object or situation, and a poem often helps readers form a picture in their mind. Poems are shorter than stories and are often written to be read aloud. Poems can be funny or serious.

Read a few poems with rhyming words aloud from books in your child's library. Ask your child if she hears any word patterns as you read each poem. Explain to her that stories can use word patterns and that word patterns are also used in poems. Many poems use words that follow the same pattern so that the poem rhymes.

Activities

Activity 1: Patterns in Poetry

Encourage your child to read the poems on the "Patterns in Poetry" sheet. Provide assistance as needed. Read each poem at least twice. Ask your child what each poem is about, and then ask her to identify words in the poems that follow the same pattern. Have her circle the words that rhyme in the same color. For example, "be" and "me" can be circled in red, and "dog" and "frog" can be circled in green. Point out that many of the rhyming words in poems are found at the end of each line.

For extra practice, repeat this activity with poems from books you have at home. Your child can point to rhyming patterns or write the rhyming words on a separate sheet of paper.

Activity 2: A Rhyming Song

Explain to your child that songs can also have words that follow the same pattern. Songs are a lot like poems. They are written to be heard, and they can be serious or funny. Sing the song, "A-Hunting We Will Go," with your child. As you sing each verse, pause and let her guess which rhyming word might come next. Sing the song again, pausing after each verse, and ask her to recite the words in each verse that follow the same pattern.

<u>A-Hunting We Will Go</u>
Oh, a-hunting we will go,
a-hunting we will go.
We'll find a fox,
Put it in a box,
And then we'll let it go.

Oh, a-hunting we will go,
a-hunting we will go.
We'll find a whale,
Put it in a pail,
And then we'll let it go.

Oh, a-hunting we will go,
a-hunting we will go.
We'll find a frog,
Put it on a log,
And then we'll let it go.

Oh, a-hunting we will go,
a-hunting we will go.
We'll find a fish,
Put it on a dish,
And then we'll let it go.

After you've finished each verse, ask your child to brainstorm other animal names. Then ask her to think of words that rhyme with each name. Let your child write another verse to the song and record it on the page called "A Rhyming Song." Then she can illustrate the new verse in the box provided. *Examples*: *snake* and *lake* or *pig* and *twig*.

When your child finishes her verse, reread the book, *Bear Hugs*. Leave out the second rhyming word in the pairs that match and see if she can guess the word that goes in the poem.

Activity 3: My Music

Listen to or sing some of your child's favorite songs. As she hears each song, ask her to identify words that rhyme. She can record the rhyming words and then circle the parts of the words that follow the same pattern. Provide assistance with spelling. Identify words that rhyme and follow the same letter patterns, as well as words that rhyme but are spelled differently.

Activity 4: Handwriting

Let your child write another line from the song, "A-hunting We Will Go," using *We'll find a* ____ *put it* _____ *and then we'll let it go.*

Wrapping Up

Conclusion
Discuss how poems and songs have rhyming words that follow patterns. Ask her to explain how to find rhyming words.

Life Application
As you listen to songs throughout the week, encourage your child to identify the words that follow the same pattern.

Lesson 4: Sentence Patterns (2 Days)

Getting Started

? Questions to Explore

- Where can we find patterns?
- What are some examples of patterns?
- How can numbers, shapes, and words form patterns?

📖 Facts and Definitions

- Sentences follow patterns.
- **Naming words** are for people, places, and things. We call these words **nouns**.
- **Action words** describe what a person or thing is doing. We call these words **verbs**.
- **Sentences** begin with a capital letter and end with punctuation, such as a period.
- Some sentences follow the pattern of a person, place, or thing word (naming word) followed by an action word.

⊙ Skills

- Identify words that name persons, places, or things and words that describe actions (LA)
- Name the ordinal positions in a sequence such as first, second, and third (M)
- Use words such as "before" or "after" to describe relative position in a sequence of events or objects (M)
- Use sentences to convey ideas (LA)

✂ Materials

- ✓ blank paper
- ✓ scissors
- ✓ lined paper
- ✓ simple picture books

Introduction

If your child is not familiar with the word "sentence," explain that sentences are words put together to communicate ideas and information. We speak in sentences and we write in sentences. Explain to your child that he has been writing or copying sentences in his lessons. Show your child an example of a simple sentence. Explain that a sentence starts with a capital letter and usually ends with a period. Try to find examples of sentences your child has written or copied.

Show your child examples of simple sentences in easy-to-read picture books. Explain to him that sentences also follow patterns. A common sentence pattern is one where there is a word for a person, place, or thing followed by an action word. An action word describes someone or something doing something. We call a person, place, or thing a noun. We call an action word a verb.

Share the following examples with your child and then ask him to recite a few sentences that follow the same pattern. As you read each sentence, point out the person, place, or thing and the action word.

- The boy jumped high.
- The dog barked loudly.
- The man ran down the street.

Note: Your child has been copying and or writing sentences all year. With this practice, most children naturally hear and have an intuitive understanding of what a sentence is. This lesson explains the terminology and the parts of the sentence. Children should be encouraged to speak in complete sentences when they communicate, which should make writing in complete sentences second nature.

Activities

Activity 1: Making Sentences

Choose an option for your child to complete. In Option 1, the nouns and verbs are illustrated, and in Option 2 the words are not illustrated.

Option 1

The activity page, "Making Sentences" (Option 1), has a list of people, places, things, and action words at the top of the page. Each word is illustrated. Let your child cut out the words or copy them. The bottom half of the sheet has sentence patterns. Your child can fill in the sentence pattern using a variety of different subject/verb combinations. Encourage him to read each sentence he forms aloud to see if it makes sense. He can also extend the sentences as he shares them aloud. For example, "The *dog eats...* its food from the bowl."

Option 2

The activity page, "Making Sentences" (Option 2,) has a list of people, places, things, and action words at the top of the page. Let your child cut out the words. The bottom half of the sheet has sentence patterns. Your child can fill in the sentence patterns using a variety of different subject/verb combinations. Encourage him to read each sentence he forms aloud to see if it makes sense. He can also extend the sentences as he shares them aloud. For example, "The *dog eats...* its food from the bowl."

Activity 2: Acting Out Sentence Patterns

Make up simple sentences with your child's name as the subject. As you say each sentence, ask him to tell you the naming word (person, place, or thing — in this case his name) or noun and the action word (verb) in each sentence.

Here are some examples:

- James ran as fast as he could.
- James played with his toys.
- James drew a beautiful picture.
- James read a book.
- James sat down.

Now you can act out different situations and your child can make up sentences that describe what you are doing. On lined paper, he can record a sentence that describes what you are doing, or can dictate a sentence that you write and he copies. Then and ask him to circle the noun (naming word) and underline the verb (action word) in each sentence.

Sample ideas:

- Fold clothes (Mom is folding the clothes.)
- Type on the computer (Mom is typing on her computer.)
- Open a door (Mom is opening the door.)

Next, let your child act out different situations, and you can make up simple sentences that describe what he is doing.

© Copyright 2019 Epiphany Curriculum, LLC

Do not copy or distribute without written permission from Epiphany Curriculum, LLC.

Page 43

Day 2

Activity 3: Completing a Sentence Pattern

Choose an option for your child to complete. Option 2 is more advanced.

Option 1

Part A:

Review the idea that sentences form patterns and that many sentences follow a pattern of a naming word (called a noun — person, place, or thing) followed by an action word (called a verb). For this activity, your child will read each sentence from the "Completing a Sentence Pattern" (Option 1) sheet aloud, and then he will decide which word completes each sentence. Review the idea that all of the sentences follow the same pattern: person, place, or thing followed by an action word. Next, ask him if the word he chose to complete the sentence is a person, place, or thing.

Part B:

In this section, ask your child to read each sentence aloud and to circle the action word that makes sense in the sentence.

Option 2

Part A:

Review the idea that sentences form patterns and that many sentences follow the pattern of a naming word (person, place, or thing) followed by an action word. For this activity, your child will read each sentence from the "Completing a Sentence Pattern" (Option 2) sheet, and then he will decide which word fits in the blank to complete the sentence pattern. Review the idea that all of the sentences follow the same pattern: person, place, or thing followed by an action word. Ask him if the word he chose to complete the sentence is a person, place, or thing and then he can circle the action word in the sentence. Explain that the noun that tells what the sentence is about is called the subject of the sentence, and the verb that tells what the subject does is called the predicate of the sentence.

Part B:

These sentences are missing the action word. Your child can decide which action would best fit in the blank. Then he can write the action word in the blank.

Part C:

These sentences are missing a noun and a verb. Explain that the subject and the verb are missing from these sentences. Ask your child to use a subject and verb to complete the sentences.

Activity 4: Sentences in Books

Read through some simple picture books. Ask your child to identify sentences. Remind him that a sentence starts with a capital letter and usually ends with a period. Let him point to the beginning letters and the periods in a few sentences.

Next, you can point out simple sentences in the text. Be sure to find sentences with just one subject and one action verb. For each sentence, ask your child to identify the noun and the verb. Let your child copy a few simple sentences from books so that he can underline the noun and circle the verb.

Activity 5: Noun and Verb

Cut five pieces of paper in half vertically. On five strips, ask your child to list common nouns and on the remaining five strips, he can list five verbs. Pick up one noun and one verb. Hold them up and ask your child to make up a sentence that uses both words. Continue with other subject/verb combinations. You can extend this activity by adding additional nouns and verbs.

Activity 6: Handwriting

Ask your child to write or copy two sentences and to underline the naming word and the action word in each one.

© Copyright 2019 Epiphany Curriculum, LLC

Do not copy or distribute without written permission from Epiphany Curriculum, LLC.

Page 44

Wrapping Up

Conclusion

Ask your child to explain the sentence pattern that he worked with today. Ask him to give you examples of words that name people, places, and things as well as examples of action words.

© Copyright 2019 Epiphany Curriculum, LLC

Page 45

Do not copy or distribute without written permission from Epiphany Curriculum, LLC.

Lesson 5: Story Patterns

Getting Started

? Questions to Explore

- What are examples of patterns that can be made and/or found?
- Where can we find patterns?

📖 Facts and Definitions

- Stories have a beginning, middle, and end.

⊙ Skills

- Recognize the beginning, middle, and end of a story (LA)
- Use words such as "before" or "after" to describe relative position in a sequence of events or objects (M)
- Predict what comes next in a pattern (M)
- Discuss, illustrate, or dramatize a story or poem (LA)

✂ Materials

- ✓ colored pencils or crayons* (Activity 2 - Option 2) ✓ glue* (Activity 2 - Option 1)
- ✓ paper* (Activity 2 - Option 1) ✓ scissors* (Activity 2 - Option 1)
- ✓ simple storybook

Introduction

Review the idea that a pattern is made up of parts that follow in the same order. Patterns can be made up of objects, words, or symbols, or they can be made up of things that happen. For example, when you get up in the morning you might follow the same pattern each day:

- Get out of bed first
- Get dressed
- Eat breakfast
- Brush their teeth

Ask your child to describe her pattern in the morning. Ask her to write about or illustrate her morning routine. She can select the 3 or 4 most important activities. Explain that storybooks also follow a pattern. Stories have a beginning, middle, and end.

Activities

Activity 1: Finding a Story Pattern

Find a short storybook that your child has not heard before and read it with your child. After the beginning of the story, ask her what she thinks will happen next. Then, before you read the ending, ask her what she thinks will happen at the end. Talk about the important events of the story. After you read the story, ask her the following questions:

- What happened at the beginning of the story?
- What happened in the middle of the story?
- What happened at the end of the story?

Discuss the idea that there might be many different things that happen in the middle of the story. You can repeat this activity with one or two additional books. Encourage your child to read a book and identify an event that happens in the beginning, the middle, and the end.

Activity 2: Story Pattern Boxes

Option 1

For this activity, read the short story on the "Story Pattern Boxes" (Option 1) page to your child, encouraging her to follow along. Then she can cut apart the pictures. On a separate sheet of paper, she can glue the pictures in order and write *beginning, middle,* and *end* in the boxes beneath each picture. She can then dictate a sentence to describe each event.

Option 2

For this activity, encourage your child to read the short story at the top of the "Story Pattern Boxes" (Option 2) page; provide guidance as needed. After she has read the story twice, she can complete the boxes at the bottom of the page. In the first box, she will illustrate and describe what happened at the beginning of the story. In the second and third boxes, she will do the same thing for the middle and end of the story. She can also write or dictate and copy a sentence for each part of the story.

Activity 3: My Own Story

For this activity, your child will create her own short story. Tell her to think of who will be in her story. Explain that we call the people or animals in a story the characters. Discuss that a short story must have a beginning, middle, and end. On the sheet, "My Own Story," she can dictate a story to you. Ask her to think about what will happen at the beginning, middle, and end of the story. Then record her story, encouraging her to stay focused on her ideas. Let her attempt to read her story when she finishes, providing assistance as needed. Then she can create story boxes by illustrating her story and/or she can act out the story using puppets, dolls, or stuffed animals.

Activity 4: Handwriting

Let your child copy or write a sentence from the story she created.

Wrapping Up

Conclusion

Ask your child to describe the pattern that a story follows.

Life Application

As you read stories with your child and tell her stories, encourage her to describe the beginning, middle, and end.

© Copyright 2019 Epiphany Curriculum, LLC

Do not copy or distribute without written permission from Epiphany Curriculum, LLC.

Page 47

Lesson 6: Sound Patterns

Getting Started

? Questions to Explore

- What are some strategies for finding patterns?
- Where can patterns be found?

📖 Facts and Definitions

- Sounds can form patterns.
- We often call sound patterns **rhythms**.

⊙ Skills

- Predict what comes next in a pattern (M)
- Extend a pattern (M)

✂ Materials

- ✓ glass
- ✓ musical instrument
- ✓ music
- ✓ spoon

Introduction

Ask your child which of his senses he can use to find patterns. Ask him if he thinks he can hear a pattern. Tell him to close his eyes and listen. Make the following sound pattern for your child to hear:

Clap, stomp your foot, clap, stomp your foot, clap, stomp your foot, clap, stomp your foot

Tell your child to open his eyes, and ask him if he heard a pattern. Ask him what type of pattern he heard (ABAB, AABB, or ABC). Then ask him to name the two sounds repeated in the pattern (stomp, clap). Explain to your child that sound patterns are rhythms. Clap a number of different rhythms and ask your child if he hears the rhythm pattern in each one, and then ask him to clap the same pattern.

Activities

Activity 1: Do You Hear a Pattern?

For this activity, your child will listen to the sound pattern and then extend each pattern. You will need a spoon and a glass for this activity. Make the following pattern for your child:

Clap, tap glass with spoon, tap glass with spoon, clap, tap glass with spoon, tap glass with spoon

Now ask him how many times you clapped and tapped the glass for each part of the pattern. Start the pattern again and give your child the spoon to use to extend the pattern.

For the next pattern, use instruments such as a drum, rhythm stick, or maraca. Tap your foot, play the instrument twice, and continue the pattern. Give your child the instrument and ask him to extend the sound pattern.

Activity 2: Listen Carefully

For this activity, your child will listen to a variety of patterns and describe each part and the order of the pattern. Your child will record the number of times each sound was made in the pattern.

Make the following sound patterns:

Slap (2X), clap (2X), stomp (2X)...

To increase the level of challenge, create more complex sound patterns for your child to identify. For example, you might use sounds to make an AABBBCC pattern or an ABBCCC pattern.

After your child listens to each pattern, he will identify one segment of the pattern and record how many times each sound repeats itself in a segment. Continue to repeat the pattern until he can identify the repetition.

Using the lines on the "Listen Carefully" page, let him record the second pattern below after listening to it. He can either copy the words at the top of the page, or use the first letters of each rhythm word (**S**lap, **C**lap, **T**ap).

Pattern:
Tap your toes (2X) Slap your leg (1X), Clap (2X)...

Let your child practice making different sound patterns using his body and musical instruments. Using the page, encourage him to record a pattern he creates and then try to imitate each pattern.

Activity 3: Music and Patterns

For this activity, play different types of music and make patterns with simple movements for the songs. Let your child identify the patterns you create and repeat them to the rhythm of the music. The "Chicken Dance" and the "Hokey Pokey" are fun movement patterns set to music.

Activity 4: Handwriting

Let your child write about a sound pattern he heard today. For example, *I heard a pattern that went...*

Wrapping Up

Conclusion

Ask your child how he can use his sense of hearing to identify sound patterns. Ask your child to describe how to make a sound pattern.

Life Application

Listen to music and ask your child if he can identify any sound patterns. Point out sound patterns that you hear in the music.

© Copyright 2019 Epiphany Curriculum, LLC

Do not copy or distribute without written permission from Epiphany Curriculum, LLC.

Page 49

Lesson 7: Making Sound and Action Patterns

Getting Started

? Questions to Explore

- What are examples of patterns that can be made and/or found?
- How can numbers, shapes, and words form patterns?

📖 Facts and Definitions

- Different sounds can be combined to form patterns.

⊙ Skills

- Create and extend patterns with actions, words, sound, and objects (M)

✂ Materials

- ✓ glue
- ✓ scissors
- ✓ paper
- ✓ variety of musical instruments

Introduction

Ask your child how sounds can be used to make patterns. Ask her to provide an example. Tell her that today she is going to be making patterns with sounds and actions.

Activities

Activity 1: Musical Patterns

Provide your child with a variety of instruments (tambourine, rhythm sticks, recorder, drum, harmonica, etc.). If you do not have instruments, you can make instruments with household items. A drum can be made with a pan and a spoon. A maraca can be made by filling a toilet paper roll with rice and putting aluminum foil on each end held on with a rubber band. You can find more ideas for homemade instruments on the Internet.

Making Your Own Instruments
www.movingbeyondthepage.com/link/558
This link has instructions for making your own instruments.
http://www.nancymusic.com/PRINThomemade.htm

Your child will create different patterns with the instruments. She can come up with her own, or you can provide guidance by suggesting some of the patterns below:

- Use two instruments to make an ABAB pattern
- Use three instruments to make an ABC pattern
- Use two instruments to make an AABB pattern
- Use three instruments to make an AABCC pattern

Activity 2: Creating a Sound Pattern

Choose an option for your child to complete. The first option is intended for children who are not strong readers and/or are visual learners. The second option is best suited for strong readers who do not require visual cues to read.

Option 1

On the "Creating a Sound Pattern" (Option 1) page, your child will cut out the sound words (and pictures) and put them together on a separate sheet of paper to form patterns. She will need to repeat each segment of each pattern twice. Ask her to perform her sound patterns or to listen to you as you perform the sound patterns she created. Check to make sure she made a pattern that repeats itself.

Option 2

On the "Creating a Sound Pattern" (Option 2) page, your child will cut out the sound words and put them together on a separate sheet of paper to form patterns. She will need to repeat each segment of each pattern twice. Ask her to perform her sound patterns or to listen to you as you perform the sound patterns she created. Check to make sure she made a pattern that repeats itself.

Activity 3: Creating Action Patterns

Explain to your child that actions can also form patterns. Play a game called "Do What I Do." Tell your child that you are both going to take turns forming patterns from actions. One person makes the pattern while the other watches closely and repeats the pattern. Continue each pattern until your child is able to mimic it. Then let your child make up an action pattern for you to copy. Some examples of action patterns are provided below:

- Pat your head 2X, tap your shoulders 2X (AABB)
- Touch your toes, touch your knees, touch your head (ABC)
- Arms up, arms out to the side, arms in front (ABC)

Ask your child to make up a second action pattern and repeat the activity.

Activity 4: Handwriting

Ask your child to write or copy a sentence that describes a pattern she made today.

Wrapping Up

Conclusion

Ask your child what it means to have a pattern made from sounds and a pattern made from actions. Let her demonstrate examples of each type of pattern.

If time permits, let your child select an instrument to make from the website found in Activity 1.

Life Application

Listen to different styles of music. Encourage your child to listen for patterns in sounds. The simpler the rhythm, the easier it is to hear music patterns.

Final Project: Patterns Video (2 Days)

Getting Started

? Questions to Explore

- Where are patterns found?
- How can sounds, words, and motions form patterns?
- What are some strategies for finding patterns?

⊙ Skills

- Identify and describe patterns (M and S)
- Recognize and describe shapes (M)
- Use props and pictures to support spoken messages (LA)

✂ Materials

✓ device to play music   ✓ video camera or digital camera that takes video

Introduction

Tell your child that people make videos to remember events and to share events with others. Some professional journalists and photographers take pictures and videos of events so that they can share them with people who were not able to see them. This is what we see on the news. We learn new information by watching videos of events.

Explain to your child that, for the final project, he will create a video of sound, word, and action patterns. First, he will locate a variety of patterns. Remind him that the patterns he has explored are made up of parts that repeat themselves in the same way. He will make a video of the patterns, describe the patterns, and share that video with others so that they can learn more about different kinds of patterns. If you have a child who has an interest or talent in drama, encourage your child to move beyond the script to make the video more creative and dramatic.

Activities

Day 1: Patterns Video

Review examples of patterns your child needs to find or create for the video. Let your child consider how to represent each pattern on video.

- Action
- Sound
- Rhyming
- Story

It might be helpful to direct him to books and music. He can also look through activity pages in the unit. The important thing is that he locates or makes up his own example of each type of pattern.

When he locates or creates an example of each type of pattern, ask him to describe it. On the four "Video Script" pages, he can write or dictate a script for each pattern that he will use in his video. On the script sheets, he will record the type of pattern, where he found the pattern or how he made it, the parts of the pattern, and how the parts create each pattern. If the pattern does not fit the exact structure of the sheet, feel free to change the script's wording. Help your child record his ideas. Then let him practice what he will say on the video to share each pattern.

For the word/rhyming and book patterns, he can read the words from a book or poem and explain the pattern. For the sound pattern he might need a music playing device (or the Internet), or he may want to make up his own sound pattern with simple instruments or sounds he makes with objects. Toys with music can also work great for this because they often repeat the same music again and again. For the action pattern, he will probably want to make up his own actions or use an action pattern from the lessons and then perform it for the video.

Day 2

Today your child will fill out the last sheet for his patterns video and will practice until he is ready to be recorded.

Let your child practice multiple times sharing each pattern he will include in the video. You can pretend to be videotaping so he gets used to looking at the camera. He can use examples from activities and books for his video.

When your child feels comfortable, you can record the video. Stop between each pattern so that he can prepare his materials and review what he will say. Let him watch the video. Ask him what he thinks he did well and what he thinks he can improve.

Wrapping Up

Conclusion

Let your child show his video to friends and family so that they can learn more about finding different types of patterns. Tell your child what you enjoyed about his video.

Unit 3: Patterns in Your World

In this unit, your child will explore patterns all around him. He will learn to sequence events using growth patterns, understand that night and day happen because of the Earth's rotation, examine patterns in dates and seasons, and apply patterns to counting and graphs.

For the final project, your child will create a mini-books about different types of patterns and then assemble the books in a lapbook that he can share with friends and family.

Vocabulary

Review vocabulary daily to achieve mastery.

word	definition
life cycle	the pattern of growth that humans, plants, and animals follow
Earth	the planet on which we live
rotation	to spin in a circle
routine	something that is done in the same way over and over again
cause	what makes something happen
effect	what happens as a result of a cause
symmetrical pattern	an object that can be folded in half to show two sides that line up with each other

Unit Review Sheet

These facts and definitions should be mastered throughout this unit. This page can be used for periodic review and study as you are finishing the unit and in the future.

Lesson 1: Patterns in Nature
- Patterns can be found in nature.
- Patterns in nature can be made of lines and shapes that repeat themselves.

Lesson 2: Patterns of Growth
- Humans, plants, and animals follow patterns of growth.
- A **life cycle** is the pattern of growth that humans, plants, and animals follow.

Lesson 3: Night and Day
- The Sun comes up during the day and goes down at night.
- **Earth** is the planet on which we live.
- The Earth spins in a circle once a day. We call this a **rotation**.

Lesson 4: Daily Routines
- A **routine** is something that we do in the same way over and over again.

Lesson 5: Calendar Patterns
- There are 12 months in a year.
- There are 7 days in a week.
- There are about 4 weeks in a month.

Lesson 6: Seasonal Weather Patterns
- The seasons and months of the year follow a pattern.
- The months are connected with different seasons and weather.
- The seasons are connected with different types of weather.

Lesson 7: Patterns at Home
- Patterns make the world more interesting.

Lesson 8: Symmetrical Patterns
- When a **symmetrical pattern** is folded in half, the two sides line up with each other.

Lesson 9: Counting Patterns
- Counting by twos is a pattern for counting objects.

Lesson 10: Tracing Patterns
- You can trace a pattern to make the same outline again and again.
- Stencils help people create patterns.

Lesson 11: Patterns in Graphs
- Patterns can be found in graphs.
- **Data** is the information that can be shown on a graph.
- Graphs are created using data.

Lesson 1: Patterns in Nature

Getting Started

? Questions to Explore

- Where are patterns found?
- What kinds of patterns can be made and found?
- Where can patterns be found in nature?

📖 Facts and Definitions

- Patterns can be found in nature.
- Patterns in nature can be made of lines and shapes that repeat themselves.

⊙ Skills

- Activate prior knowledge before and during the reading of text (LA)
- Identify and describe patterns (M and S)
- Practice reading simple texts (LA)
- Observe and describe animals (S)

✂ Materials

- ✓ *Pattern* by Henry Pluckrose
- ✓ crayons or colored pencils
- ✓ scissors* (Activity 2 - Option 1)
- ✓ blank paper
- ✓ glue* (Activity 2 - Option 1)

Introduction

Ask your child if she has seen a pattern outside. If so, let her explain the pattern. Review the idea that patterns can be found everywhere. Explain to her that over the next couple of weeks, she will discover all kinds of patterns that can be found in her own environment.

Activities

Activity 1: Understanding Nature Patterns

Read aloud pp. 1-11 of *Pattern* by Henry Pluckrose. The first couple of pages describe what a pattern is, and the rest show some common patterns found in nature. Ask her to identify and describe the pattern in each picture.

When you are done, ask your child the following questions:

- Were there any patterns that you had seen before? Which ones?
- Were there any patterns you had not seen before? Which ones?
- Can you think of any other patterns in nature that could be added to the book?

Next, ask what types of patterns she has seen when observing animals, plants, bugs, and other objects in nature.

© Copyright 2019 Epiphany Curriculum, LLC

Do not copy or distribute without written permission from Epiphany Curriculum, LLC.

Page 56

Patterns in Nature
www.movingbeyondthepage.com/link/6953
This website from National Geographic contains high-quality nature pattern photos. You may want to browse and share some of the images with your child.
https://yourshot.nationalgeographic.com/tags/pattern_in_nature/#popular

Activity 2: Patterns in Nature

This activity has two options. In Option 1, your child will cut out pattern samples and paste them on the appropriate animal. Option 2 requires her to create patterns of her own and may involve her looking in books or online to view animal pictures. Choose an option for your child to complete.

Option 1

For this activity, your child will cut out each square pattern sample from the "Patterns in Nature" (Option 1) sheet and paste it on the animal where the pattern would be found.

Option 2

On the "Patterns in Nature" (Option 2) pages, let your child create a pattern on each animal pictured. She can look in books or on the Internet to locate pictures of each animal if she needs help with the patterns.

Activity 3: Drawing Nature Patterns

Look at a variety of pictures with plant and animal patterns on the Internet or in books. You can view the images at the links provided or use a search engine to find particular types of nature patterns (such as trees, deserts, or butterflies). Ask your child which patterns are the most interesting and beautiful. Let her draw a picture of the 3-5 of her favorite patterns and and label them. Encourage her to color her pattern the same colors as the picture.

National Geographic — Plant and Flower Patterns
www.movingbeyondthepage.com/link/6954
https://www.nationalgeographic.com/photography/photos/patterns-flora/

National Geographic — Animal Patterns
www.movingbeyondthepage.com/link/6955
https://www.nationalgeographic.com/photography/photos/patterns-animals/

Activity 4: Handwriting

Ask your child to write or copy a sentence from today's reading.

Wrapping Up

Conclusion

Review the idea that patterns can be made up of lines and shapes that repeat themselves in a regular way. Ask your child to share examples of patterns that can be found in nature. Encourage her to think about patterns not only on animals but also on other objects in nature.

Life Application

Point out patterns in nature as you come across them.

Lesson 2: Patterns of Growth (2 Days)

Getting Started

? Questions to Explore

- Where do we see patterns in everyday life?
- Where are patterns found in nature?
- Do living things follow patterns?
- What kinds of patterns can be made and found?

📖 Facts and Definitions

- Humans, plants, and animals follow patterns of growth.
- A **life cycle** is the pattern of growth that humans, plants, and animals follow.

⊙ Skills

- Record observations about parts of plants (S)
- Sequence events (S and LA)
- Write labels (LA)

✂ Materials

- ✓ bean seeds or sunflower seeds
- ✓ crayons or colored pencils
- ✓ pictures of your child at different ages
- ✓ small rocks
- ✓ clear plastic cup
- ✓ glue
- ✓ scissors
- ✓ soil

Introduction

Ask your child how he is different now from when he was a baby and a toddler. Look at pictures of your child at different ages. Explain that all plants, animals, and people follow specific patterns of growth. We call these patterns life cycles. **Life cycles** are circular patterns that follow the same processes of growth over and over from one generation to the next. Different types of plants and animals may follow different life cycle patterns.

Activities

Activity 1: A Plant's Pattern of Growth

For this experiment, you and your child will plant bean or sunflower seeds. Follow these directions:

1. Cut the top off of a clear plastic cup.
2. Punch small holes in the bottom of the cup. Explain that the holes allow water to drain properly.
3. Put small rocks in the bottom of the cup.
4. Fill the cup about 2/3 full of soil.
5. Plant the seeds about 1 1/2 inch down in the soil.
6. Put the cup in a window and add water regularly (according to the directions on the seed package).

Discuss what plants need to live and grow (dirt, water, and sunlight.) Different types of plants need different amounts of sun and water. Your child can record the plant's growth pattern by drawing a picture of its progress on the activity sheets, "A Plant's Pattern of Growth." He can also write a sentence that describes each picture and how the plant is changing.

Activity 2: Label Plant Parts

On the "Plant Parts" sheet, your child will label the parts of a plant using the words in the box. If he does not write words, ask him to identify the initial letter of each plant part, sound out the word, and record the first letter of each word on the diagram.

Activity 3: Investigating Plants

Take your child to the park or backyard to look at different plants. Identify different parts. Pull up some small plants or weeds to show your child what roots look like. Let him draw examples of three different plants that he investigates.

Day 2

Activity 4: Growth Patterns

Discuss the idea that a life cycle is the pattern of growth that a living thing goes through. Offspring of animals follow the same growth pattern as their parents.

For this activity, your child will cut apart pictures of a plant, an animal, and a person from the "Growth Patterns" sheet. Explain that all people grow and follow the same pattern, all dogs follow the same pattern, and most plants follow the same pattern of growth. Humans start off as babies, and then they become children, then teenagers, and finally adults. This process repeats itself in the same way for every person. This is the human life cycle.

Explain that most plants start out as seeds in the ground. They grow roots in the soil, and then they begin to grow beyond the soil. Some plants grow very tall, and some grow flowers. Let your child cut the pictures apart and glue them on a separate piece of paper in order from the plant's first stage to its last stage. He will also paste in order the life cycle of a person and a dog.

To extend this activity, ask your child if he can think of any animals whose life cycle follows an unusual pattern. A butterfly and a frog have unique life cycles. Ask your child what makes these animals' life cycles unique. Discuss that the babies are completely different from the adults. A caterpillar changes into a butterfly over the course of its life cycle, and a tadpole changes into a frog. Ask your child to illustrate the stages of growth for one of these animals. If he is not familiar with the life cycles of these animals, the following websites provide great information.

Life Cycle Stages
www.movingbeyondthepage.com/link/6316
http://www.tooter4kids.com/LifeCycle/Stages.htm

Life Cycle of Butterflies and Moths
www.movingbeyondthepage.com/link/6317
http://www.kidsbutterfly.org/life-cycle

The Monarch Butterfly Life Cycle
www.movingbeyondthepage.com/link/6319
https://youtu.be/jS9FbRVLeJg

Frog Life Cycle Video
www.movingbeyondthepage.com/link/6320
https://youtu.be/_YCpfzl0B4M

The Life Cycle of a Frog (Interactive)
www.movingbeyondthepage.com/link/6318
http://www.harcourtschool.com/activity/science_up_close/212/deploy/interface.html

Activity 5: My Growth Pattern

Give your child pictures of himself from birth to present. Let him organize the pictures in order from youngest to oldest. Ask him to guess his age in each picture. Talk about the pattern of growth that all people go through from birth to adulthood. Discuss what stages your child has gone through and how he will continue to grow until he is an adult.

Activity 6: Writing Words

Let your child write each of the following words five times each: *plant, grow, part*. Model writing each word for your child, and then let him copy the words.

Wrapping Up

Conclusion

Ask your child to describe the growth pattern of a plant and a person.

Note: Children will study life cycles in greater depth in the 7-9 level of Moving Beyond the Page.

Lesson 3: Night and Day

Getting Started

? **Questions to Explore**

- Where are patterns found?
- Where do we see patterns in our everyday lives?
- Where are patterns found in nature?

📖 **Facts and Definitions**

- The Sun comes up during the day and goes down at night.
- **Earth** is the planet on which we live.
- The Earth spins in a circle once a day. We call this a **rotation**.

⊙ **Skills**

- Understand that night and day occur because of the Earth's rotation (S)
- Recognize the position and motion of objects (S)
- Identify properties of objects (S)
- Write letters of the alphabet (LA)
- Record dominant consonant letters (LA)
- Write from left to right (LA)

✂ **Materials**

- ✓ basketball
- ✓ flashlight
- ✓ golf or ping-pong ball
- ✓ tennis ball
- ✓ crayons or colored pencils
- ✓ globe or basketball
- ✓ masking tape

Introduction

Ask your child how she knows when it is nighttime and when it is daytime. Ask her what kinds of things happen during the day and what kinds of things happen at night. Ask her if she knows why we have day and night.

Activities

Activity 1: The Sun, the Moon, the Earth

Show your child a picture of the Sun in a book or on the Internet. Then look at pictures of the Earth and Moon. Explain that the Sun is a big ball of fire that is very hot. Show your child a picture of the Moon and explain that the Moon is a large rock. Next, show your child a picture of the Earth and explain that the Earth is a planet.

Discuss where the Sun, Moon, and Earth are located in relation to one another. Explain that the Earth revolves around the Sun. Find a basketball to represent the Sun and a tennis ball to represent the Earth. (Explain that in reality the Sun is much, much larger than the Earth.) Have your child hold the basketball while you walk around her in a circle. Explain that this is a simulation of the Earth revolving around the Sun. Then explain that while this is happening, the Moon is also revolving around the Earth. Get a golf ball or a ping-pong ball to represent the Moon. Ask another family member to move in a circle around the person holding the tennis ball (the Earth) while the person holding the tennis ball moves around the basketball (the Sun).

On the sheet, "The Sun, the Moon, the Earth," there are three pictures for your child to label. When finished, she can then color the pictures.

Activity 2: Night and Day Pattern

Explain to your child that the Earth is constantly spinning, even though we cannot feel it. Put a ball on your hand and spin it. Explain that this movement is called rotation. Tell her the ball is rotating.

The Earth Rotating
www.movingbeyondthepage.com/link/6321   Show your child this video of the Earth rotating.
https://youtu.be/W4PM9ZEP19A

A globe will work best for this experiment, but you can also use a ball the size of a globe (such as a basketball). On the globe, put a piece of tape on the United States. (If you have a ball, draw the U.S. on a sheet of paper, cut it out, and tape it to the ball.) Explain to your child that this is the place on the Earth where she lives. Spin the globe slowly in a circle. Tell your child that each day the Earth makes one complete spin. It takes the Earth 24 hours to make one complete rotation. This is why our days are 24 hours long. Ask your child to spin the globe around one time and stop.

Take the globe and a flashlight into a dark room or closet. Explain that the flashlight represents the Sun. Your child can hold the flashlight about a foot away from the globe; tell her she can't move because the Sun stays in one place. Turn the globe so that the flashlight is shining on the tape. Explain that when the U.S. is facing the Sun, it is daytime. Spin the globe slowly until the light from the flashlight is no longer on the tape. At this point, it is night. Spin the globe a few more times and ask your child to describe when it is daytime where she lives and when it is nighttime.

After the experiment, explain that night and day is an ABAB pattern. First it is day and then it is night. Next it is day and then it is night. The same thing happens in the same way every day as the Earth rotates.

Explain to your child that the Moon is a large rock. It does not have fire and does not produce its own light. It reflects the light of the Sun, and this is why we can see the Moon shine at night. Even though we can't see the Sun at night, it is still producing heat and light.

Activity 3: During the Day and at Night

Before beginning this activity, ask your child to think about some activities that are associated with day and some that are associated with the night. Review the idea that, because the Earth follows the same pattern each day, we have our lives organized to fit the pattern. Some activities must be done when it is light outside, while other can be done when it is dark.

Ask your child the following questions:

- How would it be different if it were light all the time?
- How would it be different if it were dark all the time?

Give your child the sheets called "During the Day" and "At Night." She will draw a picture of something she does only during the day on the first page. Then, beneath the picture, she will record or dictate a few sentences that explain the activity. On the "At Night" page she will focus her drawing and sentences on a nighttime activity.

Wrapping Up

Conclusion

Ask your child to explain the pattern of night and day.

Life Application

Point out activities your child participates in during the day and ones she participates in at night.

Lesson 4: Daily Routines

Getting Started

?   Questions to Explore

- Where do we see patterns in our everyday lives?
- Do living things follow patterns?
- Where are patterns found?

📖   Facts and Definitions

- A **routine** is something that we do in the same way over and over again.

⊙   Skills

- Sequence events (LA)
- Place events in chronological order (SS)
- Recognize and describe patterns (S and M)

✂   Materials

- ✓ blank paper
- ✓ glue
- ✓ crayons or colored pencils
- ✓ scissors

Introduction

Review the idea that the Earth spins in a circle and that its position to the Sun creates the pattern of day and night (light and dark). Explain that each day, our lives also follow predictable patterns. We call these patterns **routines**. Routines are activities that we do over and over again in the same way and often at the same time of day or night. Talk about some of your child's routines.

Activities

Activity 1: My Morning Routine

Explain to your child that his life follows a pattern. Each morning, he probably does things in a similar way. On the activity sheet called "My Morning Routine," he will find pictures of a boy following his morning routine. There is one blank space for your child to add something that he does each morning. Then he will cut the pictures apart and glue them in the correct order on a sheet of blank paper to create his own morning routine.

Activity 2: A Routine for _____

Ask your child to think of another routine that he follows on a daily basis. It could be bath time, getting ready for bed, or practicing a sport. On the activity sheet called "A Routine for _____," your child can fill in the title for the routine he will describe. Then ask him to think about the routine and break it down into four steps. He can dictate a sentence about each step or write on the lines at the bottom of the boxes. Finally, he can illustrate each step or select an object or gesture to represent each step. An example is provided at the top of the page.

Note: This activity will help your child understand and practice sequential order. This skill is important for following multiple-step directions. This skill transfers to understanding story structure as well as to following steps for solving math problems.

Activity 3: Daily Routine

Turn a sheet of paper vertically and fold it like an accordion from top to bottom so that there are 8 sections. On the left side of each section you will record the time, starting with the hour when your child wakes up and ending with the hour he goes to bed. As you go through the next 24 hours, ask your child to record important activities in words or simple symbols for a typical day. Write the time when the activity occurs. There will be space for eight activities, including morning wake-up and evening bedtime. Share the following example:

Sample Daily Routine		
7:00 am	Wake up and get ready	
9:00 am	School begins	
10:30 am	Break	
12:00 pm	Lunch	
2:00 pm	Rest time	
3:00 pm	Play time	
5:00 pm	Dinner	
8:00 pm	Story and bedtime	

Activity 4: Handwriting

Let your child write or dictate and copy a sentence that describes one of his routines.

Wrapping Up

Conclusion

Review the idea that we follow patterns every day and that we call those patterns routines.

Lesson 5: Calendar Patterns (2 Days)

Getting Started

? **Questions to Explore**

- Where do we see patterns in our everyday lives?
- Do living things follow patterns?
- Where are patterns found?

📖 **Facts and Definitions**

- There are 12 months in a year.
- There are 7 days in a week.
- There are about 4 weeks in a month.

⊙ **Skills**

- Recognize concept of calendar time (M)
- Sequence events (LA)
- Connect model, number, and word (M)

✂ **Materials**

- ✓ calendar
- ✓ glue or glue stick
- ✓ laminated calendar
- ✓ poster board

- ✓ dry-erase marker
- ✓ index cards
- ✓ lined paper
- ✓ scissors

Introduction

Show your child a calendar. Explain that another pattern in our lives is weeks and months. Seven days make up a week. Each day repeats itself in the same order every single week. Show your child the weeks on a calendar. Explain that the same thing is true for the months. There are 12 months that make up a year. Each month repeats itself in the same order each year.

Ask her to name the days of the weeks and months of the year (in order).

Activities

Activity 1: A Weekly Pattern

On the activity sheet, "A Weekly Pattern," your child will extend the weekly pattern out five more days. At the bottom of the page is a calendar week. Your child can fill in the first letter of the day of the week in the "Day" column. Then, for each day, she can dictate or record her scheduled daily activities. Some days she might not have a routine activity, while other days she might have more than one.

Activity 2: Days, Weeks, Months, and Years

Show your child a calendar and explain that each month on the calendar is made up of about four weeks, and each year is made up of twelve months.

Show your child a tally mark and explain that a tally mark represents one object or event. Let her write a number or two and then show her what the number would look like in tally marks. Show her that the fifth tally mark always crosses the previous four. Your child can fill in the chart provided on the activity sheet called "Days, Weeks, Months, and Years." In the first column, she can record the number. In the second column, she can write the number word, and in the last column, she can make tally marks to represent the number. Continue practicing numbers and the corresponding tally marks to 20 over the next few days.

On lined paper, let your child practice writing the numbers 1-10 and their number words. You can also ask her how to write tally marks for the numbers 1-10. If your child is ready, she can attempt to go higher than ten.

Show your child a calendar of the current month and let her use a dry-erase marker to put the month and the numbers on the days of the week on the laminated calendar.

Note: Calendar time will be explored in greater detail in Concept 4.

Activity 3: Writing Dates

Show your child how to write the date with the day of the week, month, and year. Let her practice this skill each day over the next few weeks. She can use a calendar to keep track of the days. She can also use the laminated calendar to identify the month, date, and weather at the beginning of each day until she reaches the end of the unit.

Record ten different dates on index cards with the day of the week, month, and year. See if your child can put them in order. To make this activity even more challenging, you can use different years on the cards.

Day 2

Activity 4: Calendar Event Patterns

Select the current month on the calendar. On the calendar, record all of the activities that your child and/or family members have planned for the month. If your child does not read, you may draw symbols to represent each activity. Some things might occur weekly or biweekly, and others might occur monthly. Do the same thing for the next two months on the calendar.

Explain that many events and activities happen at the same time, over and over again. Ask your child to look at each month to find patterns. Ask her if she sees any events that occur weekly, biweekly, or monthly. These events or activities follow a pattern. Record each pattern she finds.

Activity 5: Days and Months Poster

The sheet called "Days and Months Cards" contains the names of the days of the week and the months of the year. Let your child cut them apart. Give your child a poster board that has been cut in half. Turn one half of the poster board horizontally. Ask your child to put the days of the week in order from left to right on one side of the poster. Turn the second half of the poster vertically and ask your child to put the months of the year in order from top to bottom. Once she has them in the correct order, she can glue them onto the poster board. Review the days and months on a daily basis until your child can say them in order, independently.

Note: If your child already knows the days of the weeks and the months of the year in order and can say them independently, focus on spelling them correctly.

Activity 6: Writing Words

Let your child practice writing the following words five times each: *day, month, year.*

Wrapping Up

Conclusion

Teach your child this song to tune of "Oh, My Darling Clementine":

Sunday, Monday
Tuesday, Wednesday
Thursday, Friday, Saturday
There are seven
There are seven
There are seven days of the week.

Lesson 6: Seasonal Weather Patterns

Getting Started

? **Questions to Explore**

- Where are patterns found in nature?
- Where do we see patterns in our everyday lives?
- What kinds of patterns can be made? Found?

Facts and Definitions

- The seasons and months of the year follow a pattern.
- The months are connected with different seasons and weather.
- The seasons are connected with different types of weather.

⊙ **Skills**

- Create and extend patterns with actions, words, sound, and objects (M)
- Read a calendar (M)
- Sequence events (M)
- Identify and describe different types of weather (S)
- Observe and describe weather changes (S)

✂ Materials

- ✓ calendar
- ✓ glue
- ✓ map of the United States
- ✓ construction paper
- ✓ laminated calendar
- ✓ scissors

Introduction

Ask your child to write today's date. He can use the laminated calendar for reference. Then ask him to select the weather that describes the day and to circle it on the laminated calendar.

Ask your child if he can name the four seasons. Then ask him what types of activities and weather are associated with each season.

Explain that in the same way the days of the week and the months of a year follow a pattern, the seasons also follow a pattern. The seasons repeat themselves in the same order every year — winter, spring, summer, fall, winter, spring, summer, fall, etc.

Activities

Activity 1: Seasons and Months

Look at the calendar and discuss the types of weather associated with each season. Explain that the weather follows a pattern, too. Certain types of weather are associated with certain seasons.

Using the activity sheet, "Seasons and Months," ask your child to cut the seasons apart and put them in order. Look over the poster your child created of the months of the year in the previous lesson. Then ask the following questions:

- Which month comes after March?
- Which season comes before summer?
- Which month comes before October?
- Which month comes after January?
- Which season comes after summer?

You could also ask these advanced questions:

- What month is two months after May?
- What month is three months before July?
- What month two month before December?
- What month is three months after the first month of the year?

On the "Seasons and Months" page, ask your child to fill in the missing seasons after studying the illustrations. Then he can complete the pattern at the bottom of the page. Be sure that your child understands that the months and seasons follow the same order each year and that the pattern continues in the same way year after year.

Activity 2: Weather Geography
Look at a map of the United States with your child. Explain that different states may have different weather than others. Point out Florida and explain that snow in that state is very rare, especially in the southern part of the state. Then explain to him that the states on the bottom half of the map have warmer weather, and the states on the top half have cooler weather. Discuss the weather in your state.

Activity 3: Weather Patterns
Give your child the sheet called "Weather Patterns." On this sheet, he can record the weather word beneath the season that it describes. Discuss the illustrations associated with each month and what they symbolize. Then have your child cut apart the months. Paste the top of the page on a piece of construction paper. Shuffle the months and ask your child to paste each month beneath the season and weather pattern connected with the month.

Review the idea that the months, seasons, and weather follow a pattern that is repeated each year. Explain that the weather is not always exactly the same but that it does follow a seasonal pattern. Explain that there are three months in each season, but the seasons don't start on the first day of the month.

Activity 4: Handwriting
Let your child practice copying the months of the year.

Wrapping Up

Conclusion
Discuss the month, season, and weather your child is experiencing. Let him identify the month on the calendar, name the season, and describe the weather he has observed.

Discuss which season is found in in each month of the year. Explain that while fall does not officially start until mid-September, winter until mid-December, spring until mid-March, and summer until mid-June, people still think of September as a fall month, December as a winter month, March as a spring month, and June as a summer month.

Lesson 7: Patterns at Home (2 Days)

Getting Started

? Questions to Explore

- Where do we see patterns in our everyday lives?
- Where are patterns found?

✂ Materials

- ✓ *Pattern* by Henry Pluckrose
- ✓ crayons or colored pencils
- ✓ thick and thin markers or pens
- ✓ blank paper
- ✓ quilts with patterns

📖 Facts and Definitions

- Patterns make the world more interesting.

⊙ Skills

- Predict what comes next in a pattern (M)
- Identify patterns using knowledge of properties of objects (S)
- Engage in visual spatial activities (M)

Introduction

Ask your child if she can think of any patterns in the house. Talk about how patterns make the world a more interesting and beautiful place.

Patterns Video
www.movingbeyondthepage.com/link/6322
Share this video about patterns with your child.
https://youtu.be/-NdzJg3moRY

Activities

Activity 1: Pattern Scavenger Hunt

Read the whole *Pattern* book aloud to your child. After you finish reading, go on a pattern scavenger hunt and have your child identify the following patterns from the book. Ask her to describe each pattern she finds.

1. Checkerboard pattern (pp. 4-5)
2. Patterns in nature (pp. 6-11, 22, 25, 30)
3. Patterns on fabric, wallpaper, and/or a rug (pp. 12-13)
4. Pattern on a dish (pp. 14-15)
5. Pattern on clothing (pp.16-17)
6. A repeating pattern (pp. 18-19)
7. A circular pattern (pp. 21, 23, 25)
8. A tread pattern (pp. 26-27)

Activity 2: Patterns in a Closet

For this activity, your child will complete the patterns on the "Shirt Patterns" page. Using thick and thin pens or markers will help your child draw the patterns. Once she has finished the page, let her go to her closet and other closets in the house to find patterns on clothing.

Day 2

Activity 3: A Quilt Pattern

Ask your child if she can think of anything else in the house made of cloth that might have a pattern. Look at any pillows and quilts in your home that have patterns. Identify the patterns and discuss the designs.

Give your child the page called "A Quilt Pattern." She will color the shapes according to the directions to create a pattern. Ask her to name each shape and the number of sides and angles on the shapes. Explain that a quilt pattern can be in patches, like the pattern on the page, or it can work its way out from the center and build on itself.

Activity 4: Drawing Patterns

Draw two or three shirt outlines on a sheet of paper and ask your child to create her own pattern for each shirt or copy a shirt pattern from a family member's closet.

Next, select one of the following:

- Draw a circle on a sheet of paper and ask your child to design her own pattern for a plate. She could also copy a plate pattern from the cupboard. Encourage her to use crayons or colored pencils.
- If you have a child who is not interested in drawing, sorting silverware into patterns can be a fun activity, too. If you have a variety of patterns of silverware, your child can sort them instead of drawing a plate pattern.

Activity 5: Handwriting

Let your child write or dictate and then copy a sentence that describes a pattern found on something in her closet.

Wrapping Up

Conclusion

Review the idea that patterns can be found all around us. Discuss how patterns make the world more beautiful. Ask your child what it would be like if there were no patterns around the house and everything were a solid color.

Lesson 8: Symmetrical Patterns

Getting Started

? **Questions to Explore**

- Where are patterns found?
- What kinds of patterns can be made? Found?
- Where can patterns be found in nature?
- Do living things follow patterns?

📖 **Facts and Definitions**

- When a **symmetrical pattern** is folded in half, the two sides line up with each other.

⊙ **Skills**

- Compare and sort objects (S and M)
- Recognize and describe shapes (M)
- Identify and describe patterns (M)
- Count objects in a set (M)
- Compare numbers of objects (M)

✂ **Materials**

- ✓ construction paper
- ✓ scissors
- ✓ paint or glue

Introduction

Look closely at a picture of a butterfly's wings. Ask your child to describe the pattern in the wings. Then ask him if the wings look the same or different. Explain that the wings have a symmetrical pattern. A **symmetrical pattern** is one where you can fold something in half and the two halves line up.

Activities

Activity 1: Alphabet Symmetry

Cut apart the letter squares on the "Alphabet Symmetry" page. Fold each letter in half vertically and show your child how each half of the symmetrical letters lie perfectly on top of each other. If the letter is not symmetrical, the two halves do not line up. Repeat folding the letter horizontally.

Write other letters of the alphabet and draw the lines of symmetry. Explain that some letters are symmetrical when you fold them in half from side to side. Others are symmetrical when you fold them in half from top to bottom, and some letters are symmetrical both ways.

Activity 2: Shape Symmetry

Cut out a variety of squares, triangles, circle, ovals, and rectangles in different sizes from construction paper. Your child can attempt to fold the shapes and decide which shapes are symmetrical and which ones are not. Look at which ones are symmetrical when folded from top to bottom, side to side, and both directions. Let him draw the line of symmetry for the shapes that are symmetrical.

© Copyright 2019 Epiphany Curriculum, LLC

Do not copy or distribute without written permission from Epiphany Curriculum, LLC.

Page 73

Your child can sort the shapes into two groups — symmetrical and non-symmetrical. Then let him count the number of shapes in each group. Ask him to tell you which group has more shapes and how many more shapes are in the larger group than in the smaller group.

Activity 3: Symmetrical Art

Trace the butterfly pattern from the "Symmetrical Art" page onto a piece of construction paper. Let your child cut out the butterfly. To create a symmetrical design, he can squirt globs of paint or glue down the center of the butterfly and globs on the wings. Next, he can fold the butterfly wings in half and hold them for two to three seconds. When he pulls the wings apart, he will see a symmetrical design on the butterfly. The left side will be a mirror image of the right side.

Activity 4: Handwriting

Let your child write or copy a sentence about a symmetrical figure: _____ has _____ *lines of symmetry*.

Wrapping Up

Conclusion

Ask your child what it means for something to have a symmetrical pattern. Ask him if he were folded in half (from his left side to his right side), if his two sides would be symmetrical. Then ask him if he were folded in half at the waist if his two sides would be symmetrical. Ask him to describe examples of shapes, letters, or objects that are symmetrical and some that are not symmetrical.

Symmetry Game
www.movingbeyondthepage.com/link/6324
This game lets children complete the other side of a shape.
http://www.softschools.com/math/geometry/symmetry_game/

Life Application

Look for symmetry in different objects around the house and outside.

Lesson 9: Counting Patterns

Getting Started

? Questions to Explore

- Where do we see patterns in our everyday lives?
- What kinds of patterns can be made? Found?

📖 Facts and Definitions

- Counting by twos is a pattern for counting objects.

⊙ Skills

- Count objects in a set (M)
- Count by 2s (M)
- Write numbers 1-20 (M)
- Listen to a story read aloud (LA)
- Answer questions about a story read aloud (LA)
- Act out a story (LA)

✂ Materials

- ✓ paper clips, pennies, or counting bears
- ✓ scissors
- ✓ pennies

Introduction

Explain to your child that we can also use patterns when we count. These patterns make counting faster and easier.

Activities

Activity 1: Counting by Twos

Tell your child that the most common pattern for counting is by twos. Give your child up to 20 pennies, paper clips, Legos, or counting bears. She can practice by lining up the objects in a row and using two fingers to pull two objects toward her at a time. Count by twos to twenty together and then let your child practice independently. Write the numbers that you say when counting by two and explain that you don't say every number, only every other number.

Let your child look at the pictures of the items on the page, "Counting by Twos." Ask her to count each set of objects by twos. It may help her to use two fingers to touch two objects at a time. She can record the number of objects in each set. If your child is having trouble, she can cut the objects apart and then count them like manipulatives, putting two fingers on two objects and pulling them toward her.

Activity 2: Even and Odd Counting

Explain to your child that when she counts by twos, she is using an even number of objects. An even number is any number where the objects in the set can be paired. Give your child 6 pennies and ask her to put the pennies in pairs. Then give her eight and have her do the same. Next give her five. She will find that one penny does not have a partner. Explain that five is an odd number. Hand her three pennies and ask her if she has an even or odd number of pennies.

Write down the odd numbers: 1,3,5,7,9,11,13,15,17,19. Now, write down the even numbers: 2,4,6,8,10,12,14,16,18,20. If your child does not know odd and even numbers, encourage her to practice saying odd numbers and even numbers to twenty until she has mastered them.

Select one of the following options. If your child has mastered even and odd numbers to twenty, select Option 2. If she needs more practice in identifying even and odd numbers, select Option 1.

Option 1

For this option, "Even and Odd Counting" (Option 1), your child will identify the missing numbers in the sets of even and odd numbers.

Option 2

For this option, "Even and Odd Counting" (Option 2), your child will identify the missing numbers in the pattern. These number patterns go beyond just finding even and odd numbers. Explain to your child that in these patterns, she must determine what is being added or subtracted to get from one number to the next number in the pattern. This activity is much more challenging than Option 1.

Number Cracker
www.movingbeyondthepage.com/link/6325
When your child finishes the activity, she may want to play this interactive game to practice finding a missing number in a pattern.
You can set the level of the game to easy, medium, or hard.
http://www.funbrain.com/cracker/index.html

Activity 3: How Many Clowns?

Ask your child to cut out the car pattern and clown faces from the "How Many Clowns?" sheets. As you read the story below, your child can keep track of how many clowns are in the car by placing their faces in the car as they enter. Ask your child to try to fill in each blank in the story.

At the circus, a clown drove up in a little car. He had another clown sitting next to him. There were __ clowns in the car. Then he honked the horn. Two more clowns jumped in, and there were __ clowns in the car. Two more clowns ran up behind the car and got in the back door. There were now __ clowns in the car. Then he drove around and picked up two more clowns. That made __ clowns in the car. Before he drove away, two little clowns shoved themselves in the front seat. I didn't know you could get __ clowns in a car.

After your child listens to the story and puts the clowns in the car, take them out and have her tell her own story about the clowns, changing the number of clowns that get in the car. Tell her that that her story should start out with one clown in the car and continue with pairs of clowns getting in the car.

If a child is ready for an extra challenge, have her start out with all the clowns in the car and then tell the story as the clowns get out of the car. Explain that her story must continue with the same pattern. As she tells the story, record the number of clowns that are in the car as the story continues. At the end, identify the pattern of the numbers you recorded.

Activity 4: Handwriting

Ask your child to write or dictate and then copy a sentence about the clowns in the car.

At this point in the year, children should be transitioning into writing their own simple sentence at the end of a lesson. Do not worry about spelling at this time, as this can add an extra level of anxiety. Identifying spelling mistakes may actually discourage writing because a child may be afraid of spelling a word wrong. At this age, children still spell phonetically since they have not had much formal spelling instruction. When a child writes a sentence, continue to reinforce the fact that a sentence needs a noun (subject) and a verb (predicate), begins with a capital letter, and ends with a period. As your child writes her own sentences, ask her to identify the subject and the verb in the sentence.

Wrapping Up

Conclusion

Let your child practice counting items in large quantities by twos around the house.

Lesson 10: Tracing Patterns

Getting Started

? Questions to Explore

- Where are patterns found?
- What kinds of patterns can be made? Found?
- How do you make a pattern?

📖 Facts and Definitions

- You can trace a pattern to make the same outline again and again.
- Stencils help people create patterns.

⊙ Skills

- Identify customs and symbols associated with holidays (SS)
- Complete spatial visualization tasks (M)
- Recognize and create a variety of patterns (M)

✂ Materials

- ✓ attribute blocks
- ✓ craft materials to decorate holiday cut-outs
- ✓ markers, glitter, paint
- ✓ scissors
- ✓ stencils or cardboard
- ✓ construction paper of different colors
- ✓ fabric, wood, or plastic
- ✓ paintbrush
- ✓ stencil paint

Introduction

Explain that when we are cutting things out, we often use a pattern. We call the pattern the "original." Then we trace around the pattern to create more objects that are the same shape as the original.

Activities

Activity 1: A Different Kind of Pattern

Explain to your child that he has been studying patterns with objects and numbers that repeat themselves in the same way. Patterns can also be models for creating or making something that looks like something else. For example, you might trace around a star to create a pattern to make a lot of stars that are the same size.

Another kind of pattern is one where you pattern something to look like something else. When people copy a design, they say that they patterned their design after the thing they saw. For example, you might see a pillow in the store and then try to make your own pillow that looks similar.

For this activity, your child will cut out heart and star patterns from the "A Different Kind of Pattern" activity sheet. Then he will trace them onto construction paper and cut them out to create multiples in different colors. On the bottom of the sheet, he will use his attribute blocks to recreate the two patterns shown. He can create the designs on a separate page, trace them, and then color them.

Ask him to practice making different objects out of his attribute blocks. Encourage him to tell a story about one or more of the objects he creates.

Activity 2: Tracing Holiday Patterns

Let your child cut out the patterns for a heart, a Christmas tree, and an egg from the "Tracing Holiday Patterns" sheet. Explain that these are all simple patterns that we can use to create holiday crafts. Ask your child to identify the holiday associated with each pattern. Tell him to create three of each object using the patterns. He can cut the patterns out and trace around them on colored construction paper to create new objects. Then he can cut out his new shapes.

After he has finished cutting, ask him to identify the original patterns. Then ask him to count the total number of shapes he has created. Review the idea that he used an "original" pattern to create objects in the same shape. Now he can decorate the shapes with markers, paints, glitter, or any other craft materials.

To extend the activity, he can use his shapes to design ABAB patterns, AABB patterns, ABC patterns, etc. For example, Egg, Egg, Tree, Tree, Egg, Egg, Tree, Tree....

Activity 3: Stencil Patterns

Tell your child that another way a pattern can be created is by using a stencil. Explain that a stencil is a piece of cardboard or plastic with a shape cut out to help you paint or draw a shape on the material underneath. Take your child to the store and pick out some simple stencils (or make your own with cardboard). Show your child a variety of stencils. Let him practice using a stencil to create designs on paper. Ask him why it would be hard to create the patterns without the stencil. Talk about how stencils help artists keep their designs the same sizes and shapes as well as helping them space the designs equally apart.

Now let him use a stencil and stencil paint to design a pattern on fabric, wood, or plastic. Ask him to think about what he wants to make. Look for ideas in magazines or on the Internet.

Activity 4: Handwriting

Ask your child to write or copy a sentence about his favorite holiday.

Wrapping Up

Conclusion

Ask your child how a pattern can be used in art. Let him explain how to use a pattern that is traced and how to use a stencil to create a pattern.

© Copyright 2019 Epiphany Curriculum, LLC

Do not copy or distribute without written permission from Epiphany Curriculum, LLC.

Page 79

Lesson 11: Patterns in Graphs

Getting Started

? **Questions to Explore**

- How can patterns be made or found?
- Where can we find patterns?

📖 **Facts and Definitions**

- Patterns can be found in graphs.
- **Data** is the information that can be shown on a graph.
- Graphs are created using data.

⊙ **Skills**

- Find patterns in graphs (M)
- Predict what comes next in a pattern (M)
- Collect and organize data (M)

✂ **Materials**

- ✓ block
- ✓ crayons or colored pencils
- ✓ leaf
- ✓ sponge
- ✓ cotton ball
- ✓ large bowl or small tub
- ✓ penny

Introduction

Ask your child if she remembers what graphs and charts are. Review the idea that graphs and charts communicate information in a picture so that the information is easier to understand.

Ask your child if she remembers any graphs she has seen or created and what information could be found on the graphs. Look at examples of graphs in previous lessons, activity pages, in books, or on the computer. Introduce her to the word *data*. Tell your child that **data** is the information used to create a graph. Point out examples of data in graphs.

Explain that one reason to put information in graphs is to find patterns in the information. Patterns in graphs show data that repeats in the same way and can help predict what might happen in the future.

Activities

Activity 1: Finding Patterns in Graphs

Look at the pages, "Finding Patterns in Graphs" and "Finding Patterns in Charts."

For the bar graph, your child can circle the title of the graph in red and circle the labels on the horizontal and vertical axes in green. Explain what each label means and the purpose of the graph. Read the title and labels to your child and discuss the data on the graph. Ask her to describe any patterns in the graph. She can color the days when John read two books orange and the days when he read three purple. Ask her how many books she thinks John would read on the Tuesday following the last Monday shown on the graph.

For the chart, your child can circle the title of the chart in red and then color the girls' names pink and the boys' names blue. She can color the boxes labeled "G" green and the ones with an "R" red.

Next, ask her the following questions:

- What does this chart tell us? (what color of shirt each child wore)
- How many types of people are on the chart? (two — boys and girls)
- How many different colors of shirts were worn? (two)
- Describe the pattern in the graph.

Activity 2: Sink or Float

For this activity, your child will conduct a science experiment and record her findings on the "Sink or Float" page. On the chart she can write *sink* or *float,* or she can just use an *S* and an *F.* For the last object on the chart, she can write in her own object. Finally, she will decide if her chart has a pattern.

She will need a large bowl or small tub for the water.

After she has finished the page, explain that this experiment is not meant to show a pattern because sinking or floating depends on what materials you choose, not the order in which they are selected.

Activity 3: Does It Have a Pattern?

For this activity, your child will decide which charts/graphs on the "Does It Have a Pattern?" sheet have patterns and which do not. To help her make her decision, encourage her to color the parts of each graph that are the same with the same color. For example, on the first graph, tell her to color the bars with one square red, two squares green, and three squares blue. The colors will help her to see the patterns. For each graph or chart that does have a pattern, she can describe the pattern — ABAB, AABB, or ABC.

Activity 4: Handwriting

Ask your child to write a sentence that describes whether an object was able to sink or float.

Wrapping Up

Conclusion

Ask your child to describe how to find patterns in graphs and charts.

Final Project: Patterns All Around Lapbook (2 Days)

Getting Started

? Questions to Explore

- Where are patterns found?
- How are patterns identified?
- What kinds of patterns can be made? Found?
- How do you make a pattern?
- Where are patterns found in our everyday lives?
- Where are patterns found in nature?

⊙ Skills

- Use props and pictures to support spoken messages (LA)
- Understand that spoken words represent written language (LA)
- Recognize that text moves from left to right (LA)
- Write capital and lowercase letters (LA)
- Recognize and describe patterns (S and M)
- Record or dictate knowledge on a topic (LA)

✕ Materials

- ✓ blank paper
- ✓ construction paper
- ✓ fabric pieces
- ✓ magazines
- ✓ markers

- ✓ brass brads
- ✓ crayons or colored pencils
- ✓ glue
- ✓ manila filing folder
- ✓ scissors

Introduction

Before you begin the final project lapbook, talk about all the different patterns your child has explored in his study of patterns. Ask him to name different types of patterns he has found in his environment.

Note: To make the lapbook more colorful and to save the time, instead of tracing some of the templates onto construction paper, you can copy the template pages onto paper in various colors and then cut them out. If you do not have access to a copy machine, you can use the white paper provided for the template pages and construction paper for the pages that can be made without a template, following the diagram.

Activities

Day 1

Explain to your child that for his final project, he will create a lapbook of patterns. Explain that a lapbook is a visual way to represent information. For this lapbook, your child will make mini-books to fit inside a larger lapbook. In each mini-book, he will include an example of a pattern.

Your child will need help assembling the mini-books and the lapbook for this project. However, make sure all the ideas about patterns included in the lapbook are his own.

Explain to your child that he will create six mini-books that each represent a different pattern:

1. One-page book — This book will include a symmetrical pattern.
2. Four corners — This book will contain fabric patterns.
3. Matchbook — A pattern from nature will be inside this book.
4. Three-flap book — This book will show the different stages of growth that make up the pattern of growth for a human or plant.
5. Wheel book — This book will demonstrate the four seasons.
6. Fan book — This book will contain the days of the week.

Activity 1: One-Page Book/Symmetrical Pattern

This mini-book will include a symmetrical pattern. Fold a sheet of paper in half and then cut on the fold. Next fold the half-page sheet. Write "Symmetrical Pattern" on the cover of the book. Inside the book, your child will draw a symmetrical pattern with half of the picture on one side of the fold and half on the other. He may need help with lining up the image on the page so that it is symmetrical. You may want to suggest a simple shape that he can trace.

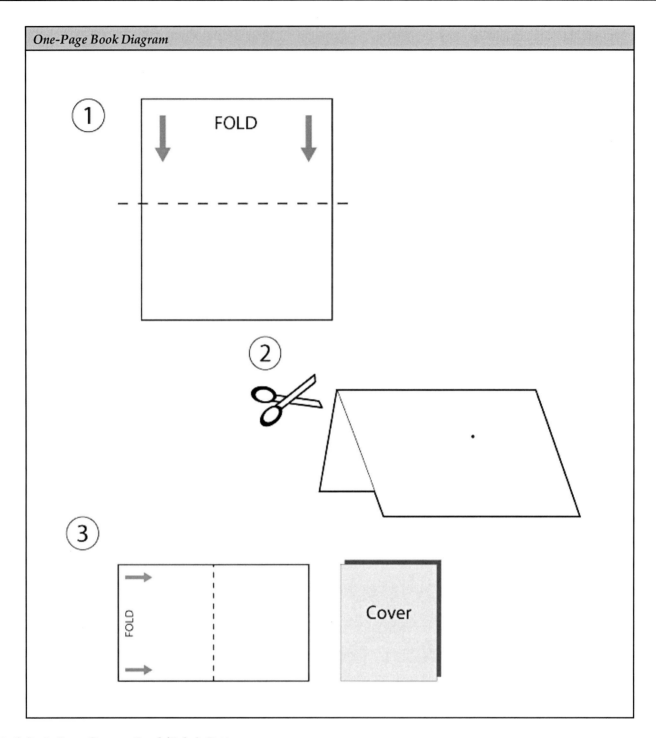

Activity 2: Four Corners Book/Fabric Patterns

For this book, cut the end of a sheet of paper off to make a square. Help your child fold the square according to the diagram provided. When the book opens, the four corners of the book will show four different fabrics with a different pattern on each fabric. You will have to cut the fabric pieces so that they can be glued on the four corners. Fabrics can be glued to the top and/or the bottom of the triangles that make the four corners.

© Copyright 2019 Epiphany Curriculum, LLC

Page 84

Do not copy or distribute without written permission from Epiphany Curriculum, LLC.

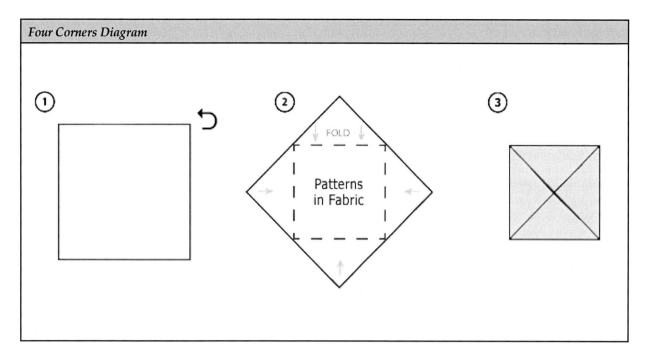

Activity 3: Matchbook/Pattern in Nature

For this matchbook, ask your child to trace the pattern from the "Matchbook Template" page on construction paper. Then help him follow the instructions on the "Matchbook" page to fold it to make the matchbook. On the inside of the matchbook, he can include a pattern from nature. You can print the pattern from the computer and let him cut it out and glue it in the book, he can cut a picture out from a magazine that shows a pattern in nature, or he can attempt to draw the pattern inside the matchbook. On the front of the matchbook, have him write "Pattern in Nature."

Day 2

Activity 4: Three-Flap Book/Pattern of Growth

The "3-Flap Book Template" page can be used as is or can be traced onto construction paper. Follow the instructions on the "3-Flap Book" page. Inside each flap, your child will show the different stages that make up the pattern of growth for a plant or human. If he chooses a human, he will include baby, child, and adult. If he chooses a plant, he will include seed, plant, and flower. On the top of the flap, he will label the stages. Then, when the flap is lifted, he can draw or cut and copy a picture of each stage printed from the Internet or cut out from a magazine.

Activity 5: Wheel Book/Cycle of the Seasons

For this book, your child will decorate the four parts of a wheel to reflect the four seasons (in the correct order). You will have to help him cut the viewing box from the top of the wheel and help him assemble the wheel according to the directions provided on the "Wheel Book" page.

Activity 6: Fan Book/Days of the Week

For this mini-book, your child will write the days of the week on the patterns provided on the "Cut-outs" page. Then he will cut them out and stack them in order. Use a brad to fasten the pages together to make a fan book. See the "Fan Book" page for details.

Activity 7: Assembling the Lapbook

Help your child assemble the lapbook according to the directions provided. Help him arrange his mini-books inside the lapbook and glue the back of them to the folder, ensuring that the mini-books still open. On the front cover flaps of the lapbook, he can write "Patterns" for the title. Then encourage him to decorate the cover with a variety of patterns.

Lapbook Tutorial
www.movingbeyondthepage.com/link/6326
For additional help, refer to this video.
https://youtu.be/WPJO-WvqoTk

Wrapping Up

Conclusion

When your child has finished his lapbook, ask him which mini-book he is most proud of and what his book teaches about patterns. Encourage him to share the lapbook with family and friends.

Summary of Skills

Language Arts

- Act out a story
- Answer questions about a story read aloud
- Discuss, illustrate, or dramatize a story or poem
- Identify words that name persons, places, or things and words that describe actions
- Practice reading simple texts
- Read or attempt to read simple text
- Recognize that text moves from left to right
- Recognize the beginning, middle, and end of a story
- Record or dictate knowledge on a topic
- Understand that letter combinations make words
- Understand that spoken words represent written language
- Use props and pictures to support spoken messages
- Use words that describe color, size, and location
- Write from left to right
- Write letters of the alphabet

- Activate prior knowledge before and during the reading of text
- Become familiar with a variety of types of books: nursery rhymes, story books, and informational books
- Identify rhyming words
- Listen to a story read aloud
- Produce rhyming words
- Recognize that spoken language has identifiable speech sounds
- Recognize that the sequence of letters represents the sequence of sounds in a word
- Record dominant consonant letters
- Sequence events
- Understand that some words begin and end alike
- Use author's model of language
- Use sentences to convey ideas
- Write capital and lowercase letters
- Write labels

Math

- Collect and organize data
- Compare numbers of objects
- Connect model, number, and word
- Count objects in a set
- Engage in visual spatial activities
- Find patterns in graphs
- Identify and draw shapes
- Predict what comes next in a pattern
- Recognize and create a variety of patterns
- Recognize concept of calendar time
- Use words such as "before" or "after" to describe relative position in a sequence of events or objects

- Compare attributes of two objects using appropriate vocabulary
- Complete spatial visualization tasks
- Count by 2s
- Create and extend patterns with actions, words, sound, and objects
- Extend a pattern
- Identify and describe patterns
- Name the ordinal positions in a sequence such as first, second, and third
- Read a calendar
- Recognize and describe shapes
- Sequence events
- Write numbers 1-20

Science

- Create patterns using knowledge of properties of objects
- Identify patterns using knowledge of properties of objects
- Observe and describe animals
- Recognize the position and motion of objects
- Understand that night and day occur because of the Earth's rotation

- Identify and describe different types of weather
- Identify properties of objects
- Observe and describe weather changes
- Record observations about parts of plants

Social Studies

- Identify customs and symbols associated with holidays
- Place events in chronological order

© Copyright 2019 Epiphany Curriculum, LLC

Do not copy or distribute without written permission from Epiphany Curriculum, LLC.

Page 88